# I'm Your Daughter, Too

## The true story of a mother's struggle to accept her transsexual child

R. Madison Amato

ISBN: 1-4700-9765-6
ISBN-13: 9781470097653

# Dedication

Dedicated to all children who have ever felt abandoned. To all parents who have felt overwhelmed. To Robert for keeping me laughing for thirty years. To Ella Ruth, Julia Ann, Edna Lou, Stuart, Tom, Butch, Roberta, Mary Margaret, Ray, Richard, Ruth Ann, Mama and Daddy for their abiding love and family support. And especially: Kristen—for her humor, Ashley—the golden one and Amy—the little Buddha.

# Acknowledgments

Heartfelt thanks to my editor, Marcia Trahan, for her guidance, support and unwavering determination to bring this to fruition. Thanks to the manuscript readers for their contributions: Carol Lorente, Mary Catherine LaFrance, Kathy DiFabbio, Ed Loughman, Marcia Gleason and Brian Gleason. For listening and crying with us: Katie Hickey, Jim Rohrer, Mary and Bill Buskey, Debbie and Brian Heelan, Kim and J.D. Smith, Patty and Eddie Keyes, Billy Muldowney, Tom Fitzpatrick, Ruth Ann Griffin and all of Rob's friends at NY State DEC. Thanks to the managers at the Empire Plan, UnitedHealthcare: Andrea Mitchell, Jens Olsen and Ginny Sandoval for their untiring willingness to make sure our claims were processed. Thank you Linda Weller, for expert electrolysis and fashion advice. Thank you Marci Bowers, MD for being a true artist and for having such a knowledgeable staff. Hats off to Trinidad, Colorado for making us feel welcome. And thanks to Thomas Grant, Ph.D of New Paltz, NY and Donna Festa at Westchester Medical Center for keeping us sane for many years.

For privacy, family names have been changed throughout the book.

# PROLOGUE

It seemed like an ordinary day in Trinidad, Colorado, but it was far from ordinary for our family. It was the day that I had feared—the day that I had railed against. And despite all my efforts to prevent the events of that day, they were upon us. We were two thousand miles from home, scared and resigned to our fate. It was surgery day, May 22, 2009. It was the day Dr. Marci Bowers would work her artistry and our son would become our daughter.

I had grieved for William for six years. I had lost sleep and twenty pounds. But I had finally accepted Angie, the little "bee-otch," as she called herself. And now, all I wanted was to get through the day and help her recover from the difficult surgery.

My husband didn't seem to share my despair. He was saddened by the changes, but just shrugged, sighed heavily and mumbled, "It is what it is."

I can't tell you how many times I had heard, "How's Robert doing? William is his only son." I always answered, "He's doing better than I am."

Robert was calm, always in control. He helped me, talked with me, and held me for hours while I cried. He comforted Angie, solved problems and corrected my mistakes. I'm sure it's partly due to his training as an emergency responder. When he arrives at the scene in that big green truck with the lights flashing and the ear-piercing WONK...WONK, the lanes clear, people step aside and his truck is escorted to the accident. He's the incident commander—he makes everything right again. He's the strong, capable leader, an everyday hero.

As we waited for the anesthesiologist in the pre-op area, I noticed that Rob was sitting very still, not talking non-stop, the way he usually does. He was staring at the ominous double doors leading to the operating room. Suddenly he jumped up. "We're going now, Angie."

"That's good." She flashed her crooked little grin and winked at me as I kissed her cheek. "I need some time alone. Don't worry. See you later."

Rob slumped onto the sofa in the stark waiting room and began fiddling with his BlackBerry. I squirmed in the straight-back chair and propped my feet up on the table. Pushing the chair onto its hind legs, I balanced precariously and rocked slowly. I stared at the clock as it ticked louder and louder. Closing my eyes, I dropped my head back and took a deep breath. I prayed. "Give me strength to get through this day."

When the BlackBerry clattered to the floor, my chair slammed down and I jumped up with arms flailing. "Oh, Robert," I whispered in dismay.

"My son, my son," he sobbed. "I've lost William." He shook uncontrollably. He held his head and swayed back and forth. He leaned forward and pounded his knees. "No! No! No!"

I touched him lightly and he slumped into my arms. "Why did this happen?" He sniffed loudly and swiped his face with his sleeve. His big brown eyes stared at me. "Why?"

He was inconsolable. I led him down the hall to the tiny chapel of Mount San Rafael Hospital. He called every friend and every family member. He cried and cried, letting go of everything he had held inside for six years. He patted my arm, shook his head slowly and shooed me away.

Reluctant to leave, I stared at his slumped shoulders, wondering how we would get through the day. Knowing he wanted to be alone in his grief, I returned to the waiting room.

Tick...Tick...Tick...Hour after hour ticked away the life of our young boy—a frail, lonely child whose epilepsy, emotional problems and sadness had consumed him, until Angie—that interloper—sneaked through the cracks of his anguish and despair.

# Chapter 1
# Angry mom

It was summer 2008, a year before the surgery. I blinked back tears as William turned slowly, admiring his reflection in the fitting room mirror. He shimmied the skimpy T-shirt over his midriff, and then stretched it down to his miniskirt, revealing the contours of the padded 34A that cradled his budding breasts. His lips quivered, rose slightly and broadened into a wide grin.

"Fits good, Mom. Now I can throw out that water balloon bra."

The five-year battle to save my son was over. I had failed to convince him that he was not a girl. Despite hundreds of hours of psychotherapy and gender therapy, after countless arguments—she had won. Angie's hatred of his male body had destroyed William. He was now sterile from estrogen injections and rendered impotent by testosterone blockers. He was chemically castrated—a eunuch, by choice.

Angie stood triumphant, hands planted firmly on her slim female hips. She flipped her long dark hair forward, then back. I imagined at any minute she might dance up to the mirror, blow a kiss and wink at herself. "Great, just great. I love them. I don't want to be too big. A or B cup is fine."

Through tears I saw a fuzzy image of my daughter: a girl developed out of the imagination of a small boy who had been broken by his difficulties. This was the girl who had been protected and nurtured by that dear boy. Then to assert herself, she destroyed him.

How could I ever love this little bitch?

Leaning closer to the mirror, she studied her dark blue eye shadow and ran her index finger along the thick black eyeliner. She flicked her eyebrow with her pinkie. "I need to have my eyebrows waxed. Can we go to the salon after we do my school shopping?"

"You need a manicure, too?"

Fingers fanned out in front of her, she wrinkled her nose, twisted her bright red mouth into a pout and slowly studied each well-groomed, bright red nail. "They look OK. I'll just polish them before we leave for school. I like my new black polish with the silver specks. Did I show you my black lipstick?" Not waiting for my reply, she continued. "I love it. Goth is so cool."

"So, then, you like the bra?"

"Love it. Love it! I thought I was goin' to wear those water balloons forever. I never knew about a padded bra. Can I get one more color? I saw a kinda greenish-blue one. 'Course, pink's my favorite color. I want to look at the panties. Thongs are the hardest to buy. I have to buy two sizes bigger 'cause I have so much to hide. Everything's got to be tucked under. What a pain! I can't wait to get rid of all that down there. I hate it so much."

"Oh God," I thought, "He still wants surgery. It's not enough that he dresses like a girl. It's not enough that he wears makeup. Why can't he be a metrosexual or a transvestite? Why can't he just be gay? What is this obsession with sex change surgery? How could a twenty-two-year-old know what he wants? When I was twenty-two I knew nothing...nothing at all. That's when I made my big mistake."

"We need to get your dorm things. Do you need a blanket?"

"I want a fluffy pink one."

I guess that didn't surprise me. Nothing he said—or she, as I was trying so hard to say—surprised me anymore. No, the surprises were over. Everything was pretty much out in the open. Nearly everyone knew, much to my chagrin.

We left the store; I held my breath as Angie approached the escalator. The spiked heels clicked a portent clanging louder and louder in my ears. My chest tightened. I raced ahead so if she fell, I'd be in front to catch her.

"I want another pair of heels just like these but a different color."

When we were about halfway down the escalator I glanced up to make sure she was still upright. She was totally relaxed, smiling, standing tall and proud. I half-expected her to wave to the crowd.

As we approached the bottom, I nearly panicked, wondering how she would get off the escalator. I quickly stepped off with my arm outstretched, bracing for the worst. Ignoring me, she headed off toward H&M. "My favorite store—I need a coat."

I collapsed on the marble bench outside the store, trying to slow my racing heart. "Is this really happening? Did we just walk through the Poughkeepsie Galleria with her wearing a miniskirt and spiked heels?" But what amazed me was, this time—unlike each outing for the last few years—no one had stared at her in dismay. I had scrutinized every face for any sign of shock, wonder, or disdain. I saw nothing except a few young men admiring an attractive girl. Had she truly transformed and now passed as a girl? "Then why can't I see it? Why, why, why?" As I had asked myself a thousand times: why did this happen to my child?

I dropped my head into my hands, trying to regain some composure. "I can handle it. I can handle it. I've been through so much worse. Maybe he'll change his mind."

I scraped my fingers through my short, wavy white hair, sighing heavily. I was aging rapidly. A year ago I gave up coloring my hair. I cut it short and let all the white grow in. I had a lot more to worry about than a skunk stripe.

I stared at my dark green, stodgy Clarks clogs. I cleaned my trifocals on the burgundy turtleneck I was wearing even though it was summer. Over the last few months my Levi's had begun to hang on my scrawny, flat butt; I was wearing insulated underwear so they wouldn't fall off. "She's all excited about a bra and I don't even need one anymore."

Angie was like a fourteen-year-old girl, which is typical of transsexuals as they begin their transition. The hormones create female adolescence with all its manifestations. She wore way too much makeup, dressed provocatively and flaunted her newfound femininity. She flirted with the bag boy at the grocery store, the cable repairman, and the neighbor—who gaped at her, trying to figure out who she was. She chatted easily with store clerks about hair, make-up, clothes and spiked heels. She had talked more in the last two years than William had his entire life. Under different circumstances, I would have thought she was a delightful young girl.

I was much too old to deal with a teenage girl. I felt like I'd been bucked off a rodeo bull. I was caught in the rope while he kept dancing and bucking and nobody would stop him. "Where's the rodeo clown? Why can't somebody capture this run-away bull and free me? Stop! Please stop this world and let me get off."

We had to finish her school shopping. I wasn't sure I could get through the day, much less through the next year until her surgery. I held out hope that this would all end, but my hope was rapidly fading. This headstrong, know-it-all girl was determined to have William's genitals cut off. "She thinks she's right about this. I don't know how she knows."

I was trying so hard to grasp what had caused this and to accept it. I desperately wanted to love her, but I was torn apart by fear and grief. I was horrified that she would willingly mutilate his body. This wasn't tattoos or piercings; nose, eyebrow or tongue rings—this was considered medically appropriate by the psychologists, the gender therapists, the endocrinologists and the surgeons.

I wasn't so sure. "How do they know it won't be a mistake?"

And yet there were times that I accepted her. I was constantly picking petals off the daisy. "He's a boy. No, she's a girl. A boy...no, a girl." I just wanted to scream sometimes. "Make up your mind! Accept her. Love her. She's told you for five years. She is a girl!"

She was excited to return to school. SUNY Cobleskill, one of the most conservative schools in New York, had assigned her a room in the girls' dorm. Did the rest of the world truly see her as female?

"Hey lady." A stranger was shaking me. "That girl is trying to get your attention."

She was at the entrance of H&M, waving me toward her. She could barely stand under the weight of the clothes. "I found lots of great tops, skirts, pants and this trench coat."

"But Angie, it's all black. You can wear so many colors."

"I only wear black. It goes with my red fishnet. I need to buy a new one, this one's gettin' ratty." Jamming her nails through holes and jerking the top up to prove her point, she grinned widely, wrinkling her nose and lifting her shoulders. "I love my fishnet."

And that, too! I ground my teeth and clenched my fists. I wanted to scream. "That damned fishnet! Why does she have to wear it every single day? Fishnet tops, gloves, stockings; red fishnet, black fishnet; torn, ratty, old fishnet—every day!"

# Chapter 2
# The tomboy grows up

Twenty or thirty years ago transsexualism was rarely discussed. I vaguely recall hearing about a soldier who had caused quite a stir in the military, and a tennis player some years back who made national news when he had a sex change. But until that fateful day in 2003, when my seventeen-year-old son told me that he wanted gender reassignment surgery, I knew nothing about transsexuals. Like most people, I viewed them with disbelief, confusion, and revulsion; back when I heard about the tennis player, it was just morbid curiosity. Today with the proliferation of information on the Internet and the media attention given to transsexuals by MTV, *Oprah*, *20/20*, Discovery Channel and *Law and Order*, transgender people have begun to emerge from society's veil of shame.

When we hear of cross-dressing, we usually think of drag queens which most of us find quite humorous, or perhaps we think of a confused child, who we assume just needs time to figure things out. But parents never, ever suspect that their child has the wrong genitals. Parents imagine every type of catastrophe that can befall a child from the moment the child is conceived. What if he has birth defects, cancer, is raped, murdered or kidnapped. We think of all of these and more, in part to try to prevent them, or worse, to prepare ourselves for them. But we can't prepare for sex change—it's beyond our comprehension to think that a boy may, in fact, be a girl. We can understand that an effeminate boy may be gay or that a masculine girl may be a tomboy or lesbian. But beyond those possibilities, our thinking about gender is limited. Most parents simply cannot prepare for life with a transsexual child.

Angie's transition changed everything about my life. It affected everyone I know—my husband, children, grandchildren, parents, siblings, every distant relative; friends, bosses, co-workers; the curious neighbor, the cable repairman and the local pharmacist. I began to reevaluate every aspect of my life from my childhood up to my own child rearing methods. I scrutinized every decision and major life event: marriage, childbirth, divorce; my spiritual life, career, pastimes; my failures and successes. I had to decide who I could talk with and how I should think about Angie. I wondered if something in my early life or in William's life had caused it. Was it genetic? Was it personality? Was I a terrible mother? Did I cause this?

Few people know anyone who has had genital reassignment surgery. But for the few who have witnessed the transition, it's a profound experience which can turn an ordinary person into a companion—willing or not—on an extraordinary journey through one of life's most difficult passages.

⌖

A few weeks after shopping for Angie's school supplies, I sat drumming my fingers on the antique mahogany writing table. I stared at the magnolia blossom on the ivory monogrammed stationery. For the umpteenth time in as many months I was trying to write to my parents. "How can I tell them about Angie? How can I tell them that their grandson is now their granddaughter?"

It was Angie's responsibility to tell family and friends. The gender therapist had given her advice on how it could be done. Angie had told all of her friends and most of our extended family, but I didn't expect her to tell my parents. No, that was my job. As I imagined it, I had to walk alone through the valley of the shadow of death. My parents would see my lips moving, they would lean toward me straining to hear my words, they would look at each other in shared confusion—but they could not possibly comprehend. Could they understand that red fishnet was the silk cocoon that swaddled an exotic butterfly? I didn't understand. How could I expect them to?

*Dear Mama and Daddy* I began, snickering at the idea that a grown woman would refer to her parents as Mama and Daddy. Robert laughs hysterically every time he hears a Southerner say Daddy. "What is wrong with you Southerners? Can't you call your parents Mom and Dad?"

Well no, we can't. Can we stop saying yes ma'am and no ma'am? No, of course not.

*So how is the weather in North Carolina? It's still lousy here in New York. I'm so sorry that William hasn't been for a visit. Actually, William is the reason I'm writing. You remember when I was a tomboy and insisted that you call me Jimmy?*

"No, no, no, you stupid ass!" I spit out each word through clenched teeth. I ripped the paper angrily into hundreds of little pieces. "Being a tomboy is nothing like being a transsexual. You just wanted to be a tomboy so you could do what boys did." I folded my arms on the desk and banged my head on my forearm over and over. I felt like a ten-year-old trying to admit that I had told a lie.

Growing up in the early 1950s it was normal for girls to want to be like boys. Those rowdy, rambunctious creatures had all the advantages. Girls were required to wear dresses to school. We had very few organized sports. We couldn't be doctors, dentists, engineers; we were denied admission to the schools simply because we were girls. It was definitely a man's world back then. Girls in the South were restricted to a limited number of life options.

In my family of four girls, we couldn't even go shopping without wearing a dress, and at times, we were required to wear a hat and white cotton gloves. My mother, like most

Southern mothers, was strict; she ruled with an iron fist. She told us how to dress, how to act, what to think and what we would be when we grew up.

As a descendent of the earliest Colonial plantation owners in Bladen County, North Carolina, I had a regimented life of church, school and family obligations. My grandmothers and all my aunts were teachers. I was expected to become a teacher, marry a professional, and of course, have children who would be named after family members. In the South and in my family especially, tradition is sacrosanct.

My grandfather, Edward William White, was a successful tobacco farmer on the land that our ancestors had settled. My mother feared and respected him. She had planned to name me Edwena after him, but then found "Rhonda" in a magazine. I preferred Edwena, so I could have been called Wendy. But no, I got stuck with Rhonda and have had to hear "Help Me, Rhonda" ever since I was in high school. My middle name, May, was my aunt's name. I guess Mama was saving Edward William for that boy that never came.

I adored Granddaddy and had named my only son after him. Mama was so excited when she found out. "I'm so proud of you. I'm sure you will rear him to be a fine young man who will follow the family traditions."

All four of us girls have family names. My older sister, Ruby Ann, is named for our grandmother. I'm second and was supposed to have been Daddy's little boy. So of course I obliged and was a tomboy called Jimmy. Then there's my sister, Jamey Lynn, named for our Daddy, James. But she wasn't a tomboy; she was a prissy little thing. And finally our baby sister, Sarah Evander, named for one of our ancestors. By the time she was born, I guess they had given up on having that boy and just gave her a boy's name. We call her Evan for short.

But we weren't called by our first names. Oh, no—it was the full name. If Mama was having one of her hissy fits, as she did quite often, we heard "Rhonda May!" (Whoever had caused the trouble was called first, and yeah, I was always called first.) "Ruby Ann!" She was the oldest, but was never in trouble. "Jamey Lynn! Say-ra Evander! You better git ova he-ah right now! I've got a switch and your bee-hinds are goin' to burn!"

We could usually outrun her. I would hightail it up the magnolia tree. Ruby Ann hid in the smoke house. Jamey Lynn was the intellectual and stood her ground. "Mama, we didn't do anything!" Her blue eyes shot daggers and her long blonde braids slapped both sides of her face as she shook her head angrily. "I'm goin' to tell Daddy that you are bein' mean again." Sarah Evan, being the baby and spoiled, just flopped down and cried.

By then, Mama, who was no bigger than a minute, was huffin' and puffin' and we would come out of our hiding places and gather 'round her and have a good laugh. "Can we have some Kool-Aid?" I asked, to try to break the tension. She'd give in, having forgotten what she was so mad about. When she wasn't looking, I'd grab the forsythia switches and hide them behind the aviary that held her hundreds of parakeets. Those switches could sting, Lord have mercy.

I'm fairly sure that my family life was typical of the South in the early '50s. Although back when we kept hearing all about dysfunctional families, I began to wonder if we could have been included in that category since Mama had those hissy fits—but I just put that thought right out of my mind. Naw! We were just high-spirited 'cause Mama had that feisty French ancestry mixed in our mostly English heritage—that 'splains it!

I did all the normal girl-things beginning with cheerleading at age five, when Teeney Byrd and I were the mascots at St. Pauls High School. I played the sticks in the rhythm band, took piano lessons, studied ballet, joined the swim team and Girl Scouts, attended summer music camp at

Fort Caswell, and quite often I had terrible fights with my sisters over who was Grandmother's favorite. Since I was the middle child, I figured that I was the center of attention and perhaps the center of the whole world.

We didn't call her Grandma, or Nana. Oh no, we had to call her Grandmother. When you're the matriarch you get to be called whatever you want. Sarah Evan said that she wanted to be called "Your Highness." Jamey Lynn, who's now an ordained minister, wanted to be called "The Reverend." Ruby Ann, bless her dear sweet heart, preferred, "Grandmother." And I said, "I want to be called for supper whenever we're having fried okra." They called me a smart aleck.

Daddy was an accountant and the VP of a small railroad that served Fort Bragg, a huge military reservation near Fayetteville, where we lived from the time I was eight. Mama was a full-time homemaker.

Mama said I was a real pistol and quite a handful. She loves to tell the story of the Christmas that I stomped all my dolls 'cause I had asked for cowboy guns with a double holster. I must have gotten them for my birthday because I've seen pictures of me all decked out in a cowboy outfit with those guns. I spent a lot of time at the homeplace in Tar Heel following around my cousin, Brian, and shooting cans with his .22. My favorite outfit was a flannel shirt, overalls, (or overhalls, as we called them) cowboy hat, and cowboy boots. We dressed just alike. He was like the brother that I always wanted.

And they tell me I was real funny, which I had a hard time believing during Angie's transition, since I couldn't remember the last time I thought anything was funny. It must have been a long, long time ago when I lost my sense of humor.

"Come on, Rhonda May; show Granddaddy your peanut butter joke." They say I always obliged, showing how the peanut butter stuck to the roof of my mouth, or telling him some silly story. They say he would laugh at my jokes for hours.

Whatever happened to that little girl?

When I was in junior high, I was a page for the North Carolina House of Representatives. In high school I was a cheerleader, was in the Homecoming Court and a finalist in the Miss Fayetteville High School beauty contest. By then I had traded in my cowboy boots for English riding boots. I rode this cute little horse that balked at most jumps, sending me through the air without him. I spent a lot of free time hanging out in the stables at Fort Bragg and Southern Pines.

Daddy sent me to UNC-Chapel Hill to find a husband, so I obliged by marrying a graduate of the medical school. Big mistake! That's when my idyllic life ended and I began a downward spiral which spanned nearly four decades. I married the wrong man and then moved all the way across country to Oregon where I was totally alone. What was I thinking?

Based on my own mistakes and immaturity at that age, I could not possibly think that William at twenty-two was capable of making a wise decision. I was determined to do everything in my power to prevent him from following through with his plans to have genital reassignment surgery.

But as it turns out, I was the one who needed to grow and change. I was the one with unresolved problems and demons that needed to be exorcised. He had a lot more to teach me than I could have ever taught him.

# Chapter 3
# Husband from hell

"Breathe Mrs. Robinson. Deep breaths, OK now, pant. Come on now, you have to relax." The nurse held my hand through each contraction. "They're pretty regular now—it won't be too much longer."

"Has my husband called?" I demanded frantically.

"We've been paging Dr. Robinson all day. I'm sure he'll be here soon. I'll go check the nurses' station to see if they've heard anything."

It was winter 1977 in a small town in Oregon. I had driven myself to the hospital and now lay staring at the bright ceiling of the labor room. I pounded my fist slowly over and over on the bed. When I heard my husband's voice at the nurses' station, I turned my head to the wall and tears welled up in my eyes. I clenched my fists till the nails cut my palms.

"I'm sure you've done an outstanding job of caring for her. I've been so worried. I knew I shouldn't have gone to that clinic this morning, but they're short-staffed and I couldn't refuse." I imagined his dark eyes sparkling behind his thick glasses. I was sure he was probably touching the nurse's arm paternally as he crooned his singsong dribble. "Thank you for trying to reach me. I'll commend all of you to your superiors. I know she was in the best of care."

The door of the labor room opened slowly, and then clanged shut. I continued to stare at the wall squeezing the balled-up sheets through a contraction.

"Well, well," the sinister singsong croon began. "So you're almost a mommy—again."

I was breathing hard, bracing my body against the pain.

He leaned against the door, chuckling softly. "I had a good tennis game. Well, it would've been, if those silly nurses hadn't kept paging me. Did you want something from me? I told you I didn't want kids."

"Why didn't you tell me before I got pregnant, maybe before we got married?"

His face contorted into an ominous grin. He held a hand out in front of him and cleaned his nails with a pocket knife.

"Get out! Get out!" My screams brought the nurses running. I was tearing at my gown, trying to get out of bed.

"Should we sedate her, Dr. Robinson?"

"I'm so worried about her. I'll find her obstetrician." He paused in the doorway, a fiendish grin spreading across his face. He pointed at me. "I'll find a way."

Two days later he and Crystal, our three-year-old, came to get Allison and me. But he didn't bring the comfortable Saab. He was driving his beat-around-town old bumpy truck.

"Where's the car?" I searched the parking lot in dismay.

"I took it home. Crystal wanted to ride in the truck, so get in."

---

"She's such a lovely little girl, Mrs. Robinson. Don't you want to hold her?"

I obediently took the pink bundle from the older heavyset woman and continued to gaze out the living room window. "Does it always rain here?"

"From September till about May, but you'll get use to it. Oregonians are ducks." She hurried from the room, lightly dusting the furniture as she left.

"Give me the baby," demanded my husband charging into the room. "I hired that nurse to take care of her. We're going out."

"No. I'm much too tired. I don't want to."

He snatched Ally out of my arms and grabbed my elbow. "You don't have a choice."

⚜

Having no interest in the movie, I stared at the floor, wringing my hands.

"Look at it!" He jabbed his elbow into my ribs.

Suspended by barbed wire, the nude woman moaned softly. Her dark matted hair hung over her bruised shoulders. Blood oozed from gashes on her face. The wire snapped, dropping her into a bath tub. A heavy boot wavered over her, rose slowly, and then stomped...

I screamed and jumped up from my seat. Holding my hands over my mouth, I staggered from the theater with my husband close at my heels.

"They're not actors either," he hissed. "It's real."

I gagged and vomited on the sidewalk. "You're a sick bastard! You need help. You're demented!"

"No, not me," he sneered. "You need help, but there's no one to help you. No way out. You try to leave me and something will happen, something real bad. So don't even think about it."

⚜

I stared at the medical school diplomas on the psychiatrist's wall. "I'm afraid that he'll do something to me or to the girls. I can't sleep. I can't eat."

"Now, now, my dear," began the white-haired psychiatrist, peering over his wire rimmed glasses. "You're just very tired. You need to get a good rest. You're working on your masters. You just had a baby. Your husband is very busy with his medical practice. I know it's tough, but you're letting your imagination run away with you."

"No, no, that's not true. He's dangerous."

He raised his eyebrows, smirked, made steeples with his hands. "You know that's not possible," he said drumming his fingers on the desk. "Forget about it. Keep busy. Do things. Put it all out of your mind. Bake a cake. Run."

"Run?"

"This is Oregon. Everyone jogs, it's good therapy."

A few days later, mid-afternoon, I was still in bed. "Mommy," whispered the chubby little figure as she patted my long dark hair and smoothed the lace pillows. "Mommy, please get up and play with me."

"I'm sorry, Crystal. I'm just so tired. Donna is here with you and Ally, maybe she'll play with you."

My precocious three-year old pulled herself up tall. She slapped her hands on her hips and stared at me. A sneer spread across her face. "I hate you. You never do anything with me. I hate you!" She held her head high, chin stuck out, curly brown hair fell down her back. With arms held straight down, she turned abruptly. The Oshkosh overalls and pink shirt blurred as I watched her march from the room. She slammed the wooden six-panel door behind her.

I forced myself out of the antique mahogany bed. I welcomed the comfort of my cotton turtleneck and bulky sweater. Slowly I pulled up my size 4 jeans, which were now way too big. I crept down the stairs to the living room. Then I stood staring at my stick-thin figure in the gilt-framed mirror over the French marquetry sideboard. "Oh, Mama, why are you in my mirror?" I pulled my dark brown hair out of the straggly top knot, letting it drape over my bony shoulders. Dropping onto the upholstered Henredon sofa, I stared at the crystal chandelier.

"You really have to eat something today, Rhonda," said Donna pushing the tea cart ahead of her into the living room. She limped slightly but held her head proudly. Hanks of light hair covered the pock marks on her face. Mama had found her working for a family friend and had sent her out to Oregon to help me. Behind her, Crystal bounded in, still munching a piece of toast.

"Mommy, Donna made your favorite. Eggs, grits, and bacon. It's real good. Please eat." She knelt by the down pillows on the sofa and slowly stroked my cheek while making funny faces and trying to make me laugh.

"Thanks, Donna. Maybe I can eat later."

"Not later, Rhonda, now. You're no bigger 'an a minute. You can't lose any more weight. That baby's only three months old and you've already lost more weight than you gained."

⊶⊷

A few months later I summoned all my courage and stood with head held high and teeth locked in a death vise. He folded the newspaper slowly onto his lap. He pulled off his glasses revealing the scowl. "Oh really, now, just like that. You're getting an apartment and taking the kids. And how, may I ask, will you support yourself?"

I glared at him. "I'll get some kind of job. I can teach kindergarten."

Laughing loudly, he said. "You'll fail within a year. This is Oregon, there aren't any jobs. But what do I care. I never loved you. I never wanted children. I don't know why I married you." The menace in his voice increased with each word. "But you served a purpose. Small towns want family men for their doctors and you're certainly nice arm candy." He waved his hand to dismiss me.

I turned to leave, but the malice of his final words stopped me cold. "You won't get anything. I'll destroy you if it's the last thing I do. And don't even think about getting custody, I'll prove you're an unfit mother. Three signatures is all it takes to have you committed."

Nobody in my family had ever gotten a divorce, and I didn't know how to tell my parents. So I did what I thought was right—I wrote a letter. That was a mistake. They received the letter the same day that their little dog was killed on the highway. He had somehow escaped from home and ran right out in front of a car. Mama was beside herself with grief and then she got my letter. It just put her over the edge.

But she quickly recovered, as all Southern women know how to do, and she rose to the occasion, giving me the advice that I needed. "If it's as bad as you say, then you need to worry about yourself. If you give up custody, it will only be for awhile. He'll give them back when he gets married again. He's just doing it for meanness. He's just a weak little man, trying to intimidate you. He's not going to hurt you and he definitely will not hurt those girls. Just give him some time and space."

And Mama was right. Allison came to live with me soon after the divorce. New wives tend to dislike the former wife's baby. Crystal, on the other hand, was the same age as new wife's daughter, so I guess she made a good playmate. I told myself that we had to get out one at a time. I lived nearby so I saw her as often as I could, but it took four long years before he would let her leave. And then he had to show his true colors and was cruel to her—he acted like the small minded angry little man that he was. He told her if she went to live with me that it was over between them. And he meant it. He totally rejected her.

Whenever I think back to those years, I see that I suffered terrible depression and wasn't a good mother. I remember feeling that I was simply watching myself and my children exist. I had nightmares and debilitating anxiety. I began to wonder if he was right, that I was an unfit mother and that they would be better off with him. But I knew that I loved them and that he didn't love anyone.

Today I often wonder. "Is love enough? Is it right to bring children into the world when you're not healthy yourself." I wouldn't recover from that divorce for over a decade— years after William was born. I had already damaged two children; why did I think that I should bring another child into the world?

I rented a small furnished apartment in a large Victorian home in Corvallis, home of Oregon State University. One carload of personal items was all I took. I told myself that the beautiful home with the antique furniture didn't matter. All that mattered was that I would have a life and the girls would someday be back with me.

Not that I had much of a life. He was right about one thing—there were no jobs in Oregon. I took any job I could get. Over the next six years I worked as a nurse's aide in a nursing home, answering service operator, store clerk, kindergarten teacher, day care worker, and recreation therapist in a mental hospital—the hospital in Salem, Oregon where *One Flew over the Cuckoo's Nest* was filmed. Now that was a scary job. We walked through underground tunnels carrying more keys than Bubba has strapped to his britches hanging down below his hiney crack.

I worked with the criminally insane. I heard casual comments like, "I only made one mistake. I don't know why I'm here." Well, maybe because that one mistake was that you killed both your parents. Or, another of my favorites, "When I get out of here, that bitch goin' to pay!" Really, now will that be when she comes out of the coma you put her in, or when?

And I took my psychiatrist's advice. "Run!"

I quickly laced up the Nikes and grabbed the anorak out of the armoire. Clunk, clunk, clunk I went down the wooden stairs of the Victorian house. Anxiety forced my breath out in spasms. I held my chest to try to push the pressure away. I sprinted for two blocks, and then slowed down to dodge the students walking to the college. I jogged slowly with my hands in tight fists, past fraternity and sorority houses onto the campus.

It was raining lightly. Most of the students wore Gore-Tex jackets and hiking boots. No one carried an umbrella. I dropped my hood back and lifted my head, breathing long deep breaths. I slowed my pace and opened and closed my fists. I was plodding along as I approached the music building.

The Nikes squeaked on the wooden floors of the old building. I held onto the wooden handrail, breathing heavily as I dragged each foot up to the second floor. I stood listening to the cacophony of practicing students. Beethoven's Fifth boomed loudly from a classroom.

I pushed open the door of the practice room and flopped onto the bench of the grand piano. I ran my fingers along the keys and struck a few at random. Dropping my hands onto my pants legs I wiped the rain off each finger tip. "You won't destroy me, you bastard. I'm stronger than you. I'm a Steel Magnolia, like Mama. And you're just a weak, angry little man."

I carefully placed my fingers on the piano and began to play a quiet dirge. The notes droned and the volume increased. My face began to relax; the pain and anger drained from my body. I banged harder on the keys, lifting my head to stare at the patterned ceiling. Then I dropped my hands into my lap and let the tears roll down my face.

The door opened slowly. A shaggy white-mopped head, with sparking blue eyes peeked in. His hands jerked through his tousled hair. "I knew that was you, Rhonda. Listen, we really need to get together to work up the outline for your thesis."

I nodded obediently. My voice cracked as I tried to speak. I bit my lip, shook my head and stared at the floor. "I won't be in school any longer."

"Well, well, but I thought..." He was silent, apparently waiting for a response, but then he closed the door quietly and shuffled down the hall.

# Chapter 4
# A little mad house: sixteen years off-the-grid in a barn

I met Robert in late 1978 when we were both going through divorces and were both students at Oregon State University. Robert was studying fisheries biology and working on Polish and Russian fishing boats in the Pacific Ocean. I was in a combined masters program of music, dance and anthropology and working as a recreation therapist at the mental hospital. Crystal was five and Allison was nearly two.

Rob was my neighbor and I noticed he was always emptying his garbage when I walked Ally to day care. Finally, I figured out that he planned it that way. I watched him slowly lift the garbage can lid. Allison grinned and waved to him. Was he a stalker?

One day I was scrubbing the bathtub furiously. "I can pay my bills. I can pay my bills. Crystal will be with me soon. She will! She will! You will not destroy me." I was surprised to hear the doorbell.

I answered the door to find Rob grinning widely, showing perfect white teeth. His short dark hair was neatly styled. He wore a blue Oxford cloth button-down shirt, khaki slacks and Sperry Topsiders without socks. I knew the first time I heard him say "idear" that he was from New York—Westchester County, in fact. He was holding a pie. "I made this mushroom quiche for you." He loved to cook; I subsisted on TV dinners or takeout.

A few weeks later I had a date with Mark, a nice man from work who was kind, quiet and considerate. We just dated casually. I had sworn off serious relationships. My plan was to never get married again. The doorbell rang and I hurried to the door to find Mark and Robert standing side by side in the foyer. "Oh, uh, hi, Mark. This is my neighbor, Robert."

"I won't keep you," Rob began. "Just wanted to remind you that I got that big elk on my hunt in Montana last week and promised I would make you a stew. How 'bout my place tomorrow?"

"Sure, sure," I stammered. "See you then."

A few months later I was dating a music professor from the university. One night Rob brought over grilled Spring Chinook salmon that he had caught on the Columbia River. He also brought, for the freezer, venison stroganoff that he had made from the biggest buck I had ever seen. "What was the name of that music teacher you told me about? The one you said is a good teacher. I think I'm taking a class from him? I needed an elective."

"Robert, are you going to chase off all my boyfriends? Who am I going to date? Mark doesn't come around anymore, 'cause of you."

"I guess you'll have to date me. How about goin' with me to the ballet this Saturday?"

Now, I ask you, how could I resist a man who cooks, wrestles wild animals with his bare hands and goes to the ballet? Well, not to mention that he had chased off all my boyfriends. Yep, he told the music professor that he was dating me.

And he has kept me laughing at his antics for more than thirty years.

We married in 1982. By then I had regained custody of both girls and we had found common ground. Robert wanted to be a father and I wanted to move back East to be closer to my family in North Carolina.

His family owned property in the mid-Hudson region of New York, near the town of Red Hook in upper Dutchess County. His father had begun a barn conversion but had abandoned it when Rob was a young boy. Since he was four years old, Rob's dream had been to complete the barn conversion and live on the farm.

In February 1984 we hired an auctioneer to sell all of our home goods. We made $3,000 and thought we were rich. We loaded the girls, two golden retrievers, and our few remaining belongings into the Saab, and pulling his motorcycle, we drove cross-country to North Carolina.

The girls still remember that trip as a really great adventure. They kept diaries, followed our journey on the AAA TripTik, took pictures at the Painted Desert and the Grand Canyon, and bought souvenirs that they still have today. They laughed and told stories for eleven days as we traveled from Oregon south, and then across on Highway 40 to North Carolina.

Actually, it was horrible. We nearly froze in windy Nevada. Oregon is mild all winter and we left in February without heavy winter jackets. In Texas it snowed and we had car trouble in a state that didn't know what a Saab was. We stayed in Motel 6 everywhere we could find one that allowed dogs, and the dogs peed on the legs of the beds.

I stayed in North Carolina with the girls at my parents' home in Fayetteville. Robert continued to New York to find work and settle on the property. He got a seasonal job with New York State Department of Environmental Conservation. He moved into the abandoned barn with a kerosene heater, kerosene lights, a hand-dug well, an outhouse and a few pack rats (harmless cute little rodents) who stole my earrings for years. He took another job as caretaker for a wealthy neighbor, in exchange for a carriage house where we stayed during the first two winters.

Everyone said we were insane to try to convert the barn that we should tear it down. They were right; it was a ridiculous undertaking. The barn was a mile from the highway, so the cost to bring in electricity was prohibitive. Robert was making very little money as a seasonal worker. I managed to get a job as a tax preparer, but was laid off at the end of tax season.

We put every penny into the barn. Our parents felt sorry for us and gave us money. Robert's father bought lots of the materials for the house—the roof, windows and siding. His mother bought his truck, the tractor to plow the driveway, and a bush hog which he used to make extra money.

And besides the house being horrible, we were way back in the woods where ex-convicts had been poaching deer for years. I was terrified—but word got around that a crazy Viet Nam vet survivalist and his family was living there. That certainly cut down on the riffraff. We didn't bother to tell anyone that he had been in the Coast Guard and never saw combat. What they didn't know would be good for us.

In a snowstorm Robert would plow twelve to twenty-four hours straight. The kids and I had to walk or ski the mile out to the highway. We were often snowed in and I couldn't get to work. "Come on campers, time to get moving. It snowed last night and we have to walk out. Allison, please take those sneakers off. I just said it snowed!"

"No! And you can't make me." She stood defiantly beside her big sister, Crystal, who was laughing hysterically. By then they were both taller than me, and smarter. They had both inherited their father's very high IQ.

"Face it, Mom," Crystal began. "This place is horrible and we're getting away as soon as possible. And you're pitiful; I bet as soon as you get back, you'll sleep on the sofa all day." She was right; I did a lot of that.

The girls were embarrassed by our home, with good reason. But they developed more character, fortitude and resilience than most people get in a lifetime. Crystal is now thirty-six, has her pilot's license with instrument rating and is a manager for an airline. She's working toward her commercial pilot's license. She graduated high school with honors, was awarded a full scholarship to college and is a strong, independent go-getter. She lives in North Carolina with her new-born daughter, Maddie.

Ally also finished high school with honors, graduated with a mechanical engineering degree from SUNY Maritime. She lives in Massachusetts with sons, Jim and Billy, and husband Ray.

But their success was not a result of my mothering skills. They pretty much had to raise themselves. I suffered depression most of their lives and after William was born, I'm sure I neglected them on a regular basis. They had to manage on their own through adolescence.

William, our long-awaited prince, was born in the summer of 1986. That Saturday morning I woke up early and knew the time was near. "Robert, wake up, we have to go to the hospital. We have to drop the girls off at the Fraleigh Farm."

"No, no, we can't go today, I have a load of gravel coming for the driveway."

I told my sister, Evan, many years ago that I married Robert because he made me laugh. So, I was laughing hysterically, panting through a contraction and he was planning to work on the driveway. Finally, he woke up enough to understand that the big day had arrived. He sprang into action and we were off to Northern Dutchess Hospital in Rhinebeck, New York.

# Chapter 5
# Prince of Problems

We took Will's birth in stride—at first. We sent a wire to my parents in Ghana, where they were working as missionaries. They never got it and didn't know for three months that God had answered their prayers, that we had the long-awaited prince. My parents really wanted a grandson, Rob wanted a boy and since I already had two girls, I was delighted that I had a boy. I had always wanted a brother, so I assumed my girls would like a brother. And the girls loved having a baby brother at first. They took care of him, rocked him to sleep, and played with him.

He was a good baby. But by three months of age, the troubles began. He screamed continuously, day in and day out. The girls began spending as much time as possible away from home. I was frazzled from exhaustion. Rob had so many chores and construction projects that he was at his wit's end.

Surgery corrected Will's inguinal hernia which was causing so much pain, but then he began to have seizures. One theory was that the anesthesia may have caused them. Another theory was the DPT immunizations. But we never could get a definite answer.

We were in Syracuse when he had his first seizure. Crystal was twelve and wanted to be in a beauty contest. She was dressed in a full-length gown; her light brown hair was curled and styled hanging to her shoulders. Rob had rented a tux and was to present her at the pageant. Before the evening performance we were all gathered at Denny's for a late lunch.

"Mom," Allison pulled on my arm, staring with wide blue eyes. "Why is Will turning blue?"

He was falling forward in his high chair—the spoon he had been banging clanged to the floor. I sprang to my feet and jerked him out of the chair. He lay limp in my arms. "Quick, call an ambulance! Somebody! Please call an ambulance!"

Unfortunately, that was not the only time that Will's problems interfered with the girls' lives. It was just the beginning of many interruptions. Seizures of unknown etiology, epilepsy was his diagnosis. We began seeing neurologists all over New York State. He took every medication on the market at the time. But the seizures continued, sometimes several a day.

"Come to Mommy." I watched the little towhead with a quick smile toddle toward me. He was dressed in his favorite outfit, a two-piece blue suit with a picture of a dog jumping rope. "Come on, with jumper dog. You can do it. Will! Oh, no. Will!" I rushed over to scoop up the tiny unconscious precious child that I couldn't bear to have out of my sight. "Why, why did this happen to my baby?"

He was not a rambunctious boy. He moved slowly and carefully. Up and down stairs, he stepped very carefully holding onto the rail. He was sensitive and would cry at the least scolding. But he rarely needed scolding. He would look to me for guidance before he tried anything new.

On his first day of kindergarten, he ran up to his teacher, gave her a big hug and a kiss on the cheek. He never met a stranger, so I had to be constantly vigilant. In a store he would start talking to anyone. I kept him in my sight at all times. And he was still having seizures. I worried every day when he left for school.

Often he came home from school sobbing. He would throw himself on his bed and cry for hours. "Nobody likes me," he sobbed. "They tease me. I'm different. It's the epilepsy. I hate having epilepsy."

I sat beside him, stroking his Buster Brown hair that had changed to dark brown. He had scrawny arms and legs; he was still wearing the same size 6 clothes he had worn for two years. "Let's read your favorite story."

He nodded weakly, and stared at me with his big innocent green eyes as I read the story of the "Ugly Duckling."

᠅

"Do you think I'm gay, Mom?"

I tensed. My eyes filled with tears and I stammered: "Well, why—why would you ask that?" I stole a glance at Will, who was now eight, trying to read his puzzled face.

"The kids at school say I must be gay 'cause I let Steve do those things to me."

"Well, they are wrong. You didn't let him do those things. You were only six; you didn't know what it was all about."

"They tease me all the time and make fun of me 'cause I'm so small. Why do I have to have epilepsy? And why can't I read?"

I was at a loss for words. We were crossing the Kingston-Rhinecliff bridge, heading home toward Red Hook, New York, a quaint little town about ninety miles north of New York City. My heart was breaking.

"You have a difficult life," I blurted out. "I've been thinking about something for awhile. Why don't we stop at that Taekwondo school near home and see if that's something you might like to do. Ok?"

"I guess so. Whatever."

We drove in silence. I had no idea what to say. "Did you want to talk some more before we stop? We have a little time."

"I hate my life, that's all."

᠅

Over the next four years, Master Joe Klee and his staff led a small, frightened child through the rigors of martial arts training. I knew it would be difficult and I'm a firm believer in the buddy system, so I joined also. We trained together two or three times a week and became fierce competitors, winning many trophies and medals.

"And now I'm proud to present the award to the Most Improved Taekwondo student." Master Klee's voice boomed over the crowd gathered for the belt ceremony. "This student joined us three months ago and tonight received his new rank as a yellow belt. He works hard. He has determination and he perseveres. Will, come on up, big guy."

Will slowly rose to his feet, turned to me with wide-eyed amazement, and silently mouthed the word "Wow!" He straightened the white uniform and touched the yellow belt. He held his head high, walking resolutely toward Master Klee. He stopped, lightly slapped both hands to his sides, bowed to Master Klee, and then extended his right hand with the left hand held under his arm.

"That's a nice firm handshake, Will." Master Klee placed the red, white and blue ribbon around Will's neck, and the silver triangular medal lay against the white uniform. Will turned slowly to the audience to accept applause. He waved to me and gave a thumbs up.

After the ceremony, Will stood with Master Klee to have his picture taken. "Wait, please, can Mom be in the picture with me?"

"Sure." Master Klee motioned for me to join them. Will grabbed my hand and beamed up at me with his green eyes glowing. "We're buddies, aren't we, Mom."

The day of his first competition, he slumped in the seat of the car. "How much longer?" he whined.

"About thirty minutes. We've only been driving a half-hour. It's not a bad ride."

"My stomach hurts."

"Mine too, Will. I get so nervous at a competition that I think I might throw up."

"I thought it was just me," he sighed, very much relieved. "I'm glad we're buddies."

"You and me, Will. We're going all the way to black belt. We're a team!"

The gymnasium was crowded with students from many schools, lined-up by age. Will waved good-bye and joined the eight-year-olds.

Stillness fell over the room as a military band struck up a lively march. Will stood tall. He looked around at the gymnasium filled with competitors. His face kept breaking into a huge smile. He repeatedly opened and closed his fists, slapping his sides lightly. He marched along with the group. Now and then as he passed another group, a child would touch him lightly and give a thumbs up. Will smiled broadly.

Then all movement stopped. The band began to play the "Star Spangled Banner." Will slapped his hand over his heart, stood as tall as he could, and sang loudly.

━┅┅━

I helped him strap his chest protector into place. He flopped onto the floor and pulled on the foot guards, and then I held his gloves while he pushed his hands into them. I strapped his helmet in place. He bent down and scooped up the mouth protector and grinned at me. "Now, remember the rules. Back fist to the head, kicks to the chest protector or head gear are all OK. Understand?"

He nodded in agreement and turned to face his opponent. He looked up at the tall, heavyset boy, turned back to me with wide, frightened eyes. Then he slowly turned back around.

The fight was over quickly. Dejected, he walked over to me. "No, no." I said. "Go back to the ring."

When the judge held up his little gloved hand and handed him the trophy, his eyes bulged and he started to grin. He looked so precious, yet ridiculous with his huge plastic mouth guard smile.

He ran to me and jerked his mouth guard off. "I thought I lost."

"No, you didn't lose. We have to fight by very strict rules. Your opponent didn't follow the rules. He hit you in the face and then pushed you much too hard, so he lost points and you won. You're not hurt bad, are you?" I held the ice pack up to his cheek.

He shook his head without speaking. His eyes were locked on the two fighters on top of his trophy. He ran his fingers over the metal figures and then over the marble base. He began to cry.

"Does it hurt?"

"No, I just can't believe I won...I won a trophy."

Will loved breaking boards and performing the floor patterns, which are one-sided reenactments of battles. I loved sparring. Hitting and kicking other competitors was a great release for me. We practiced together in the evenings and spent many weekends traveling to competitions.

When I was a blue belt, I had qualified for the national competition and was practicing with the black belts at the dojang. Will was watching nervously. "Mom, they're all bigger than you."

"Yeah, that's right," I said. "And all those mean guys who pick on you are bigger than you aren't they?"

Tears came to his eyes; he hung his head and shuffled his feet.

"You just watch me, little buddy. You don't have to be big to learn how to take care of yourself. You have to be fast. You have to be good. And you have to think. Always think. The battle is fought up here," I said, banging my head with my boxing glove.

"Pair up!"

My first match was with a twenty-five-year-old. He weighed a hundred and eighty pounds to my hundred and twelve. He started the match with an instant side kick to the chest. I backed up, circled, and then as he threw another kick, I jammed him with my body and gave a punch to the chest, followed by a tap on the head. He spun around aiming a hook kick to my head. I ducked just in time and countered with a fake to the head, and a chest punch, which then rolled into a back fist to the head.

"Rest!"

I glanced at Will, who had all his fingers in his mouth. He quickly gave a thumbs up and cringed before putting his fingers back in his mouth.

My next match was with a middle-aged man weighing about two hundred pounds. We tapped gloves and I backed out of his reach. He kicked toward my head but I moved quickly and stayed out of range. He lunged toward me with a punch which landed solidly on the side of my head. I spun around and nearly lost my balance but recovered and backed up. I held my gloved fists near my face and continued circling out of reach. He lunged again and I blocked. He kicked toward my head and I blocked again, jammed up his leg with my body, gave a quick punch to the chest and quickly shot back out of range.

"Rest," shouted the instructor. "Rhonda, check on your little buddy."

Will stood with his hands over his eyes. He was shaking and rocking back and forth.

"Will, it's all right. Don't cry. Please."

"He's going to hurt you. Stop it, Mom. Stop it."

"But he can't hurt me if I stay out of his way. Sometimes fighting means just staying out of your opponent's reach. Remember, I said you have to think. Come on, little buddy, don't cry."

"Are you sure you're OK?"

"I'm really OK, and someday you'll be fighting just like this with even bigger opponents. Just give yourself some time."

The martial arts school had many activities which took up much of Will's free time. There were regular talent shows which he loved and nearly always won. He danced and clowned around and loved the attention.

Will struggled with school. He had a learning disability and still couldn't read by the time he was in third grade. The school suggested that he needed one-on-one instruction. He also continued to have what were called absence seizures. He would suddenly lose consciousness and drop to the floor or he would become totally disoriented and wander around the school. Afterward he would need to sleep for an hour or two. He had taken every medication that could be prescribed, sometimes two or three at a time. We spent many hours traveling to his neurologist at Albany Medical Center. But nothing controlled the seizures or even seemed to help. School was hell for him. Finally, in desperation, I decided that if the school thought he needed one-on-one instruction, then I was the one to do it.

I homeschooled Will for third and fourth grade. Since no medication controlled his seizures and he was home with me, we decided to stop all of his medications. Without them he could finally concentrate. I used the Calvert homeschooling materials. My parents were still missionaries in Ghana at the time and had told me that the missionaries used the Calvert School. It was a good, traditional educational program.

He was triumphant when he finally learned to read. "Can I read some more today?" He eagerly grabbed his books.

"Why don't you read our prayer first? Here."

He turned the bookmark over in his hands, looking at the feathers, a camp fire, a peace pipe and a large moon. "Uncle Doug gave this to me. It's from the Sioux Indian children, isn't it?"

"Yeah, Red Cloud Indian School. Why don't you read it?"

O' GREAT SPIRIT,
Whose voice I hear in the winds,
And whose breath gives life to all the world,
hear me! I am small and weak, I need your
strength and wisdom.
Let Me Walk in Beauty, and make my eyes
ever behold the red and purple sunset.
Make My Hands respect the things you have
made and my ears sharp to hear your voice.
Make Me Wise so that I may understand the
things you have taught my people.
Let Me Learn the lessons you have hidden
in every leaf and rock.
I Seek Strength, not to be greater than my
brother, but to fight my greatest
enemy—myself.
Make Me Always Ready to come to you with
clean hands and straight eyes.
So When Life Fades, as the fading sunset,
my spirit may come to you
without shame.

"My favorite line," I said, "is, I seek strength, not to be greater than my brother, but to fight my greatest enemy—myself."

- 39 -

"I like that too," he said. "I think about that a lot."

"Why don't we celebrate your reading by baking something? Run get your cook book."

He ran back with his slim red and white book with the young boy and girl on the cover. "A cookbook for kids," he read. "What should we make?"

"You decide. You know I can't cook. You and Dad are our cooks."

"You think I could go to the Culinary Institute to be a chef?"

"If that's what you want to be, I bet you'd make a great chef. One day soon, why don't we take a field trip to Hyde Park to the CIA? Won't that be fun?"

He nodded excitedly and began flipping through the pages. "How about the cheese strata here on page forty-four?"

"Wow, I don't know how much help I'll be."

"I don't need help." He began scurrying through the kitchen, pulling out the ingredients and utensils.

# Chapter 6
# Disturbing past

We worked together on his lessons every morning, and then I drove him to school to meet with the special ed teacher for another hour. He was learning and excelling for the first time in his life.

One day he wanted to go back to school, but not to fifth grade. His friend was in the fourth grade, so we decided that he would go back to that grade. He was familiar with the material since we had already finished fourth grade, and he was more relaxed and glad to be back.

With William back at school, I thought I'd try to get a part-time job. In 1996 the job situation in Northern Dutchess County was almost as bad as Oregon had been. IBM had recently closed several offices in the area, and lots of people had been laid off. I really wanted to work; we desperately needed the money and I'm not a homebody. The only thing I have in common with Martha Stewart is that we both were stockbrokers for Merrill Lynch. Unfortunately, my timing was off: I started in 1986.

I was a museum interpreter for Clermont, the home of Chancellor Robert Livingston. I worked for an auctioneer in Red Hook. I sold furniture for Seaman's. I was a shipping manager for Paper House Productions in Woodstock. I was a recreation therapist at Ferncliff Nursing Home—all part-time, or short term; nothing provided much income.

My favorite job and the one that offered the highest potential for income was sales representative for Recycled Paper Greetings. It gave me the flexibility to work and to take care of William. My territory was Ulster and Dutchess counties.

One day I drove to historic downtown Kingston, into the main shopping area. I pulled the black vinyl bag out of the trunk and zipped through the parking lot into a large variety store. Tossing my bag into a cart, I quickly wheeled it into a storage room. Humming to myself, I pulled my work apron out and slipped it over my head. Pulling a large cardboard box off a shelf, I sliced it open and walked briskly through the store to the greeting card display.

"What the hell," I whispered. Above the six racks of greeting cards were signs posted every foot. "Clearance: All Greeting Cards 50% Off." Staring at the signs, I ran my fingers along the cards. I took two steps back, then yanked my apron off and threw it into the cart. "My cards, my cards," I muttered.

"Your company didn't notify you?" a raspy male voice cracked nervously.

I shook my head.

"It just happened yesterday. Your line was bought out in all our stores. You know how the big companies work. Their incentives are just too good to compete with. Your company has the funniest cards, but now all the lines copy them and..." He cleared his throat, ran his fingers through his grey hair, shuffled from one foot to the other. "Listen, Rhonda, you're the best damn sales rep I've ever met and if you need a reference or something, just...damn...I can remember the mess these racks were in before you started. I'm sorry."

⇥⇤

My knuckles were white from my death grip on the steering wheel. I jerked one hand up and swiped it across my cheek, sniffing loudly. "Damn, damn." Route 28 snakes through the Catskill Mountains northwest of Kingston. I turned on to a side road and headed into Woodstock. I swallowed hard, sniffed again, and then pounded the steering wheel.

Luckily I found a parking spot on busy Tinker Street. I rummaged through the McDonald's and Burger King garbage in the back seat, found a napkin and wiped my eyes and cheeks. I pulled the rearview mirror down, cringed, and shoved it away. Stepping out of the car, I pulled at my stirrup pants, brushed off my black boots, and smoothed my embroidered vest.

Opening the trunk, I took out a cardboard box and gathered samples of greeting cards, boxed stationery, calendars, magnets, stuffed toys, games, books, postcards, and puzzles. I arranged everything in the black vinyl bag, opened a notebook and reviewed several pages. Lifting the heavy bag, I held my head high, took a long deep breath and crossed the street.

At the corner I paused briefly, then pushed open the door of the gift store. I felt sickened by the incense, musk oils and floral scents. I pulled a business card from my blouse and handed it to the clerk.

"Sorry, appointments only," the purple-hair, nose-ring, gum smacker whined.

"I have an appointment with the owner."

"Well, you should've confirmed—he's out of town. Besides, we're probably closing like all the other gift stores."

I yanked at the door and escaped onto the sidewalk. I turned abruptly and walked two doors down. Pushing the door, I noticed the sign, "Clearance Sale–Going Out of Business." Surveying the candles in the shape of hands, brightly colored posters, bongs and books, I knew that I had lost one more job in my endless attempts at trying to develop a career. The incense bombarded my nostrils. I exhaled slowly and lumbered over to the greeting cards. I twirled the spinner slowly. "Working is the only thing that I'm good at, but I just can't keep a job."

"I guess you noticed the sign."

"Yeah, Toby, I did," I replied without turning around. I continued to twirl the rack.

"The cards did all right," the slight man with the tie-dyed T-shirt and the bandana around his head continued. "I just can't make it."

"You did just fine." I faced the owner and swiped my hand across my face. "Running a retail business is one of the hardest jobs in the world. I know you feel bad now, but you did the best you could do. You're not alone."

"It's IBM closing that did it," he said. "I just don't know what we're going to do."

"I don't either."

A few weeks later I was sitting in the personnel office of the local bank. The officer across the desk leaned back in his leather chair and smiled paternally. He was making little steeples with his fingers.

"Ass," I thought.

"So why did you leave Merrill Lynch?" He gave me that look which said, you can't keep a job, can you?

"It was 1987," I began. "I'd survived the crash of October 19th as well as any of us new to the business were able to. But I knew it was doomed. I never regained enough business to make it." I didn't tell him that my baby was having seizures every day and I was needed at home more than the stock market needed me.

"Well, yes, that was a shame." He looked over his glasses in a courtly statesman way.

I imagined he was telling himself that he had had the good sense to be conservative and not take such risks. And if he could be successful, I should too. I just didn't work hard enough. I realized for the first time how barren my career was. Was it possible that I was sitting there hoping against all odds to get a job as a bank teller? Had I totally lost my mind? Did I have no professional dignity at all? Was this what a college degree and years of experience came to? "I'm selling myself short," I thought. "I deserve better than this and I'll never allow myself to feel so demeaned and desperate again. Screw the business world. I'm too damn good for this crap."

"So, when can you start?"

"Next week would be great," I heard myself say, much to my dismay. And the job was as horrible as I had imagined. But I wanted to work.

⌖

I also worked part-time at a residential treatment center for emotionally disturbed children. I was beginning to feel emotionally disturbed myself. Off-the-grid living was taking a toll on me. I felt that we were chained to the house. I was in constant fear that we would have a major snowstorm and I would be trapped.

The years of dealing with Will had left me drained. I was also burdened with guilt because I had spent so much time with him and had spent so little with the girls. My first marriage and divorce had left me feeling vulnerable, fearful and depressed. During those years I was so alone and in such turmoil that I'm sure the girls were short-changed. Somehow they survived; I just wasn't sure how.

I really wanted to move from the house. We had struggled there sixteen years, just barely making ends meet. The house required a lot of maintenance, which took all of our money. It was time to have a little comfort.

Rob totally disagreed, or at least he said he disagreed. He admitted later, after we nearly divorced, that he was afraid to sell because it had been in his family so long, it would deeply upset his father. I definitely understood that on an intellectual level.

But I was losing emotional ground quickly. I was still having the nightmares that had begun with my first marriage. I would wake to the sinister voice: "You wanted to be a mommy. You're the strong one. You deal with everything. Everything! You chose this!"

I would awaken trembling and shouting. "You won't destroy me. You won't destroy me. I can get through this. I've been through so much worse. I can handle it. I can handle it."

But I couldn't handle it. I was depressed and sinking. I couldn't tread water any longer. I felt that I kept losing everything. I began to grieve over the beautiful home and antique furniture that I had given up in my divorce. I couldn't keep a job. The girls hated me because I was always depressed. Will was in therapy for the molestation. For years we dealt with the school—since it occurred on the school bus—the police, the court system. The young man was on probation and in therapy but it was no comfort. Will struggled to understand and unfortunately I wasn't much help. We both sort of drifted along together in our sadness and grief.

Rob had found a marriage counselor and they had a private meeting. Today was my turn to meet with her before we met together. "So," Elizabeth began. "You feel that you want to leave Rob."

"No, not at all. Rob's not the problem. The house is the problem. I have to get into a normal house that doesn't require so much work and money. But if I have to leave Rob to do it, I don't know what other option I have."

"You seem rather detached. Are you close to Rob and your children? Do you have friends?"

"She's pretty astute," I thought. "Maybe I can talk to her." I was staring out the small window of her office. "The window is my sign. I have a sign that I can unburden my past. This is my window of opportunity."

"I love them, but you're right. I don't feel real close to anyone. I think I have a fear of getting close. Sometimes with the kids, I feel that I can't breathe. I have so much anxiety that all I want to do is run away. I'm afraid I will either lose them, or lose myself. And no, I don't have friends. Rob's good at making friends, so I let him."

"Have you always been a bit distant with people?"

"No, I was close to my family. They tell me that I was a lively, funny kid. I don't remember it. I was popular in high school."

"Did you love your first husband?"

"I wanted to think that I did at the time, but no, I married him 'cause he was the type of man I was supposed to marry—to please my parents. He seemed like a nice person when I met him, but then later I found out he wasn't nice. Not even close."

"I find it disturbing that you seem to have had a change in your personality from growing up until you married. What happened to cause this?"

"You're right. I've been depressed most of my adult life. I'm really not myself anymore. Taekwondo has helped me with that. I've been training for four years now and one day while I was doing my floor pattern I heard myself say, 'I'm back.' And then I kept saying it. 'I'm back. I'm back.' It was like part of me had been cut off and left somewhere, and then with Taekwondo, I opened up some kind of energy pathways and allowed myself to start coming back."

"Other than Robert, have you ever been in love?"

"In love?"

"Yeah, have you ever been close to anyone?"

"Once, in high school. But you know high school isn't real. It doesn't really count."

"So, you were in love. What happened?"

"His name was Jeff. I was a sophomore, he was a senior. I had his big class ring." I waved my hand at Elizabeth and rolled my eyes. "His favorite song was 'Help Me, Rhonda.' Now every time I hear that song or somebody says, 'Can you help me, Rhonda' I feel like a dagger is going through my heart."

"Did you break up?"

"Oh, we had our rocky times, on and off, the typical stuff. We were actually broken up when...but he had written and we..." I could feel the dagger piercing my chest. "He graduated," I continued despite the pain in my chest. "And then...he went to a private military school. It was his eighteenth birthday...he was driving...they said he died at the scene."

We sat in silence. I knew it was past the time for my session to end but Elizabeth didn't move or say anything. She handed me the box of tissues and sat quietly.

Finally I said, "Do you think that's why I'm afraid to get close to people, because I'm afraid they'll die? I never, ever put that together. I always assumed it was because of my divorce, but I think it must have started with the loss of Jeff."

"I think you are onto something big and I want us to explore this in depth in our next meeting."

⌒

"I'm sure you've thought a lot about our last meeting. Have you come up with any ways to deal with this new insight?" Elizabeth got comfortable and handed me the tissues.

"Well, I was a recreation therapist and music therapy was always important. So I got out my music collection and started playing everything that was before Jeff. Then I buried his picture, the article from the newspaper about the accident and that damn record, 'Help Me, Rhonda.' I said to myself 'You have to move forward. You can't be stuck in the past.' So I started playing songs from each year forward, one year at a time. And with each song I told myself to let go of the past and to begin to hold on to what I have now. To hold my husband and children close and to not be afraid of losing them. One interesting thing I remember is that back when he died, I didn't think about how I felt, I only thought about how his mother felt since she had lost her only child. I remember feeling so bad for her, wondering how she would ever get over it. Maybe I couldn't face my own grief, and apparently I never did."

Elizabeth and I also talked a lot about my first marriage, the divorce and the lingering fears. She helped me to understand that my daughters would take their anger out on me because their father wasn't there for them. It was easier for them to blame me. They might even be afraid they would have the same depression.

"We don't know how much of depression is genetic or environmental," she told me. "We learn what we live and there could be a predisposition. Find a way to connect with them. Ask them for forgiveness."

Elizabeth encouraged me to express my feelings about living in the house with Robert. So we began to talk a lot. With her help, Rob finally admitted that he really wanted to sell the house and move. He said he had wanted to move for years, but just couldn't admit it.

So in the 1999 Y2K frenzy, we sold what is considered a prime, off-the-grid home complete with solar electricity, the latest in propane lights and refrigeration, and an artesian well that could run a hotel. The isolation of the home with its thirty acres attracted some celebrities including an actress and a top fashion model.

Today the home has been remodeled; it's beautiful and has very proud owners. It is still off-the-grid, run totally on solar power. The home is now what we envisioned. The owners have done what we would have done if we had been wealthy. With tremendous sacrifice, we achieved something really great.

It had started as an experiment to see if we could develop the isolated shell into a fully functioning home. In 1984 the Internet was not available; books and periodicals were the sources for our research into solar energy and alternative lifestyles. I spent five years researching and developing the electric and water systems for the home. We learned how to build floors and walls, and how to install windows and decks. We wired the house for DC and AC. We set up the plumbing. We started with kerosene lights, progressed to gas lights and a gas refrigerator. From a gravity fed cistern we developed a DC powered water pump which eventually supplied a kitchen, tub, shower and washing machine. We learned to conserve electricity by living on a small 1000 watt solar system.

For sixteen years we "got back to basics." We were called "pioneers" by environmentalists, "legends" by the local farmers who had taken bets that we wouldn't last more than a year, and "crazy" by everyone else.

We were fortunate enough to have a carriage apartment on our neighbor's property where we lived the first two winters. Our plan was to move into the barn after it was completed. We were researching the Amish ways and were at the local theater watching *Witness* starring Harrison Ford and Kelly McGillis who played an Amish woman. Harrison was spying on Kelly who was sponge bathing in the dim kerosene light. Rob leaned over to me and whispered, "I think we can live without electricity."

We gave up our carriage house and moved into the barn. We faced challenges and overcame difficulties that required creative problem solving skills. We learned to work together to resolve issues which had taken us to the brink of divorce. We survived a snowstorm that dumped three feet and a blinding blizzard which trapped us in our truck where we nearly died.

Our experiment was a resounding success. We felt that after those sixteen years that we could handle any challenge. But we had no idea the difficulties that lay ahead. I had never known the kind of fear, confusion and gut wrenching anxiety that I would face as William began his journey of self-discovery. I had never experienced the depths of despair that would take me to the brink of suicide.

We were leaving an extremely difficult life but we were heading straight to hell.

# Chapter 7
# Just when we thought the worst was over

We stood in the woods, prayed to the forest spirits and buried remembrances of our lives on the farm. And then we moved close to New Paltz, New York where Robert was employed with the Department of Environmental Conservation. We chose the Highland Central School district because their special education is considered top notch. Will worked his way out of special ed. By high school, he was taking all regular classes with no extra help needed. He was comfortable with school.

I stood at the kitchen window every morning wringing my hands, watching him get on the school bus and praying that he wouldn't have a seizure. Unfortunately, many days I got the call from the school nurse letting me know he was sleeping in the sick room, or he had been found wandering around the school dazed and confused.

The neurologist felt that we might be able to find a permanent solution to the seizures. He referred us to Dr. Mary Zupanc at Columbia Presbyterian Hospital who was head of the Pediatric Neurology Department and specialized in epilepsy.

In October of 2000, Will was admitted to Columbia Presbyterian for a full battery of tests, in anticipation of neurosurgery which would destroy the portion of the brain where the seizures began. He had 24/7 EEGs and video monitoring for two full weeks. I slept in a chair in his hospital room for the entire stay.

That was another one of those times when Will's problems interfered with Crystal's plans. She was due to graduate from flight school and her airline offered to fly us to the ceremony in North Carolina. She cried and begged, but as much as I wanted to go, I couldn't leave Will in the hospital alone. I felt torn between the child who was dependent on me and the adult child who had never had my attention. My guilt and sadness deepened.

But even with two full weeks of testing and medical monitoring, the results were disappointing. They showed that his seizures started in many different areas of the brain and therefore surgery was not feasible. Fortunately, there was a fairly new medication, Lamictal, which had been effective in treating his type of seizures.

He began the medication and four months later he was free of the seizures. For the first time in his life, he did not have to worry daily if he would have a seizure. At the age of fourteen he was a new person. His entire life up until then had revolved around dealing with epilepsy. Suddenly he could think clearly, and was taking a medication which had no side effects.

Soon afterward he began to do really well in school and was making honors grades. He even had a few more friends. Many times he told us that he still felt he was very different from everyone else. He said it was confusing because he had always thought he was different because of the epilepsy, but now he felt strange and didn't know why.

To reward him for his great grades and to give him an adventure, we enrolled him in a summer term at the Congressional Leadership Conference in Washington, DC. They have a very strict dress code so I spent weeks buying suits and sport coats, ties and dress shoes for him. I was amazed as I watched a very handsome young boy board that plane for DC.

He paused before going through security. He straightened the striped tie and lifted his chin high. He stroked his dark brown, neatly styled hair. His blue blazer contrasted with the starched white shirt. He stepped quickly with his wingtip shoes, argyle socks and khaki pants. Any mother would be proud to claim this young handsome boy. I imagined what a handsome man he was going to grow up to be. He looked so much like my husband. He also had that same confident swagger of his namesake, Granddaddy Edward William.

He called us a few times to tell us that he was having a really good time and that he had a big surprise for us. Rob and I drove to Albany International Airport, eagerly anticipating his return. It had been a welcome relief for the last few months that he was finally feeling good about himself. Finally we had a normal, happy son. We were waiting by the stairs at the baggage area, looking for a young boy in khaki pants and a blue sport coat. In the distance we saw a thin, ratty, dark-haired person wearing a red fishnet top, black cargo pants with metal chains and black combat boots.

"Mom! Dad! It's me. You like my outfit?"

"Oh, my," I whispered.

Apparently they had spent lots of free time at a mall and he had found his clothing style. He was very pleased and excited for a new life. He had friends all over the country and he planned to keep in touch. He was chatting easily, telling us all about his trip.

"What did you enjoy most about your trip?" Rob asked.

"We went to see Congress, and we had a mock Congress which was really fun. I found out that I'm pretty good at debate. I liked that the best. Then we did lots of sight seeing. I went to the Smithsonian but couldn't find the picture I was looking for. They said it wasn't there."

"You were looking for a picture? What kind?" I asked.

"It's this really huge painting of Joan of Arc. It's like ten feet tall. I learned all about her in school. You know, she wore men's clothes and they said it was against God for her to dress like a man. But I think she knew what she was doing. She thought it was the right thing to do."

"OK, I'm a little confused," I said. "You wanted to see the picture because she was a woman who wore men's clothes? But she's not wearing men's clothes in that picture."

"You know about that picture?"

"Yes, that's my favorite painting. Do you want me to take you to see it?"

"Oh, Mom, where is it? I saw a little picture of it and I know she's not dressed like a man but she has this amazing look on her face. She's listening to the voices that are telling her what to do. When can we see it?"

"Well, you're on school vacation for a few more weeks. Why don't we plan a trip into the city to see it? It's at the Metropolitan Museum of Art."

"That's it, oh yeah. I was thinking it was the Smithsonian. That's why I wanted to go to DC. I wanted to see that picture. I can't wait. Let's go soon."

I felt totally confused. Why was he so interested in Joan of Arc dressing like a man? That just seemed odd to me. But I was glad he was interested in art, and together we planned a trip to see Joan of Arc by Jules Bastien-Lepage.

The train station is only ten minutes from our home in Highland, New York, the Hamlet of Highland on the Hudson, as it says on the town marker. It's a tiny three corner town nestled in the hills. We drove through the village, crossed the Mid-Hudson Bridge into Poughkeepsie and parked near the train station. He had been to the city many times, but this was our first trip together.

"I'm going to see Joan, wow. She's so neat."

"She led the army, she freed France, she was burned at the stake and is now a saint. What is it about her that you find the most interesting?"

"She was a woman but she wore men's clothes," was his off the cuff response.

"I'll buy you a print that you can frame and hang in your room. I have one in my office."

"You have a print already?"

"I've had it for years. I thought you had seen it. I'm taking you to the city to see my favorite painting."

He stared out the window most of the hour and a half trip, pretending to enjoy the river and the hills, but I knew he was deep in thought. As soon as we pulled into Grand Central, he jumped up and raced for the platform.

He slowed down enough for us to enjoy a stroll through Central Park and the zoo, but he had one thing on his mind. He was eager to see Joan of Arc. "Let's go, Mom." He grabbed my hand and headed for the stairs. "You said the Impressionists, right?"

We zigzagged through the museum, not looking at anything else. We were in the large hallway by the Impressionists paintings. "OK, here we are. Walk down this hallway and she's on the right."

He approached the painting tentatively. His mouth dropped open, then shut tightly. He tilted his head from side to side. He walked up close and then stood as far back as possible. He didn't say anything; he just stared. Finally he whispered, "It's my favorite, too."

I bought him the print, which still hangs on the wall over Angie's desk. As we were leaving the museum, we stopped to admire the work of the artists on the sidewalk. There was a young girl painting calligraphy characters of names. "Can I get my name painted?"

"Sure. Let's go talk to her."

"You stay here, I'll be right back." He hurried over and talked at length to the artist. Finally, he nodded his head vigorously and clapped his hands. A few minutes later he proudly showed me the calligraphy.

"That's a lot of characters. Is it Will or William?"

He shuffled his feet, twisted up his mouth and shrugged. "Oh, it's just a nickname I go by." Quickly changing the subject, he added, "Let's walk through the park again."

A few months later he was dressing for Halloween. "You can't look yet," he yelled. "I'll be out in a minute."

I was trying to figure out why he was being so secretive this year. Usually he talked for weeks or months about his costume. It was always the usual boy thing—ghost, pirate, army guy. But this year he had been hiding in his room and sneaking things in.

"Ta-da! What do you think?"

"Oh, my, well, oh my. Will, I don't know what to say. You're dressed like a girl! Where did you get those clothes? You want to be a girl for Halloween?"

"I bought them with my bottle money. Aren't they great? I look like a girl, don't I?" He twirled around, grinning sheepishly. He held up the ends of the skirt and curtsied. He admired himself in the mirror and tilted his head from side to side.

"Well, yes, I suppose. But why do you want to look like a girl? You're a boy."

"I don't want to be a boy. I want to be a girl." He stomped his foot and glared at me in defiance. "I can be anything I want. And I want to be a girl."

"But you can't really be a girl, Will, you're a boy. It's OK to wear girls' clothes for Halloween but boys don't wear dresses." I felt totally confused. What a strange costume for him to choose. And why did he say he wanted to be a girl? Our lives had been in turmoil since he was born. How many problems could one child have?

I mentally ticked off the list of problems—epilepsy, learning disability, emotional and social difficulties, and sexual molestation. "William, you hate when the kids make fun of you. What do you think they'll do when they see you dressed as a girl? Aren't you just asking for more problems? Please, let's come up with another costume."

"I don't care what they say anymore. I hate them all. I'll do anything I want and if they make fun of me, I'll just punch 'em."

"Don't talk like that! You know as a black belt you can't just go around punching people."

He rolled his eyes and smirked. "Mom, calm down. You know I wouldn't do that. Master Klee taught me to only hit in self-defense. I'm not stupid. I'm just kidding. You take things too seriously. But I'm not wearing another costume. This is it. I think they'll like it. Besides, they call me a fag most of the time anyway; I wish they would call me a girl."

Finally, in desperation, I told myself it was no big deal. He could wear any costume he wanted. At least he wasn't moody, sad or upset the way he usually was. He wasn't worrying about what the other kids would say or do. He seemed somehow very self-satisfied and confident. Certainly he was not his usual frightened self.

He had fun that Halloween. It was such a pleasant change from the usual turbulence of his life. The kids did make fun of him, but he seemed to enjoy the new attention.

I felt very puzzled by the incident but since he didn't talk anymore about it, I just dismissed it as young kid's fun. I assumed it was just a one-day lark and after awhile, I completely forgot about it.

---

When puberty began, Will crept into a dark cave of self-loathing. I had always thought that boys couldn't wait to start shaving their beards, that having a beard was something they were all proud of. But he hated the beard and all body hair. He became withdrawn and sullen, spending all of his free time in his room. He barely talked anymore; mostly he just shrugged his shoulders, or grunted. Sometimes he would get into a long discourse on the problems he was facing. We were constantly vigilant for signs of suicide. "Does he have my depression? Is this what I've taught my child? Can't I do anything right as a mother?" I worried constantly that I had failed him.

He began to let his hair grow, but he shaved his entire body every other day. We had many discussions about being gay. One week he thought he was gay, the next week he thought maybe he was straight and then the next week he thought maybe he was bisexual, and then again the following week, maybe he was gay.

But, he didn't date anyone. Ever. No interest. He had lots of girls asking him out, and he would hang out with them but he didn't date. He also had no interest in boys. And then one day he told us, "I know I'm not gay but I don't think I'm straight either. I always felt different because of the epilepsy, but that's not why I'm different. It's something else. It's something much bigger. I just don't understand. I really need to start seeing Dr. Grant again."

He had always been very open with us, talking about everything. We were often embarrassed by how frank he could be. But this time when he began to see Dr. Thomas Grant, his psychologist of many years, he stopped talking with us. He would tell us that his sessions with Dr. Grant were good, but he wouldn't tell us anything about what they discussed.

They met regularly for three years. When Will was seventeen, he invited us to his session. He said that he needed Dr. Grant to help him talk to us.

Robert and I were waiting in the car. William had asked us to come into the office for the last fifteen minutes of his session. "So, how do you feel about him being gay?" I asked Robert.

"I don't have a problem with it. The most important thing is that he's happy with himself. He's a sweet, good kid.

He's doing well in school. At least now that he's finally going to admit it, he can get on with his life."

"I agree. I know it's difficult for him to talk about or admit. I suppose the experience he had with Steve is still very upsetting for him. Maybe now he's reconciled all of that. I've suspected it for years and he's talked about it for years. Maybe he just needs Dr. Grant to help him talk about the future more openly. We probably should go in now. And then we can all get on with our lives."

I was eager to finally begin the discussions that would set him on a course to accept himself and his life. I was so glad that he was talking to us and that life would settle down into some kind of normalcy. "At least it's not going to be a shock; we know what he's going to say. We know he's gay, don't we?"

We walked the short distance through the bank parking lot to the front of the small tan house on Main Street in New Paltz. We clomped up to the top floor and sat staring at the carpet listening to the whir of the fan that gave the counselors and patients their privacy. "It's going to be alright," I thought.

"Come in, please," said Dr. Grant. He ran his fingers through his short black hair and adjusted his thick glasses. "Glad to see you both. William has requested that we talk with you, so I'll let him begin."

I held my breath and looked at Will, who was fidgeting in his seat. He took a long deep breath and slowly exhaled. "First of all, I want you to know that Dr. Grant and I have been discussing this for several years and he agrees with me." He picked lint off his black cargo pants and then jammed his fingers in the sleeve of his fishnet top, lifting it up to examine the torn, ratty material.

"God made a mistake with me." He paused, coughed and stared at the floor. "You see, he gave me a penis, but I'm not a boy. I'm really a girl. I've felt like a girl for a long time. I hate my body. I can't stand to look at myself...and

I want to have sex change surgery to fix God's mistake." He looked from me to Robert, back at me and then at Dr. Grant.

My gasp echoed through the small office. The whir of the fan outside in the hallway pierced my ears. I glanced at Robert, who was leaning forward in his chair with arms crossed staring at the floor. I was fighting back tears. My mind was racing.

Ever since that day, whenever I've thought about our meeting, a cute, catchy song by Deana Carter always comes to mind. It's called "Did I Shave My Legs for This?" I looked at Will and thought, "I sent you to therapy for this?" I looked at Dr. Grant who was nodding in agreement, and thought, "I paid you money for this?" I was dumbfounded and bewildered. "I sacrificed my life for this? I raised a boy for this? Did I shave my legs for this?"

Dr. Grant coughed nervously and began. "William has what is called Gender Identity Disorder. It's quite rare but it's very real, and his body is not in line with his perception of himself, or herself, as it is. I feel strongly that she should begin therapy with a gender therapist and I'll be glad to help you locate someone."

I nodded silently, and shuffled in my seat. "So maybe a gender therapist can convince him that this is a mistake. At least there's hope," I thought. "We'll get to the bottom of this. I bet it's from the molestation. Damn that kid. Damn the school. They let him back on the bus even when they knew what he had done to other kindergarteners. Will this nightmare ever end?"

Dazed, confused, numb and lightheaded, I followed William and Robert out of the room. Clomp, clomp, clomp. We plodded down the wooden stairs. The clomping beat louder and louder. We were marching to a different drummer, and this drummer was banging the death drum. I wanted to break free and run...run...run!

# Chapter 8
# What is gender?

My husband and I are total opposites. Robert is gregarious, loves to eat, loves spur-of-the-moment activities, isn't much for planning ahead, could rival Robin Williams in a stand-up comedy routine and was once rushed by autograph-seekers who mistook him for Con Hunley after a concert.

I am too-serious, a true loner; I think too much, hate surprises, can't eat if I'm upset and when I was younger looked like Emmylou Harris. Now I look like a skinny Paula Deen. I plan out everything to the tiniest detail, make endless lists, and fall apart in a crisis. The year preceding Angie's surgery, Robert gained fifteen pounds and had a potbelly. I lost twenty pounds and looked anorexic.

From the day we met with Dr. Grant and learned of Will's desire to have surgery, I questioned everything. I did not believe he was a girl. I did not understand why he couldn't just dress up like a transvestite now and then, or why he couldn't just forget about this obsession with sex change surgery and accept himself as a boy. Why couldn't he just be gay?

Robert, on the other hand, was calm, assured, accepted everything, and thought it would all work out for the best, no matter what. His favorite saying is, "It is what it is."

I had never even heard of the term transsexual until a few years ago. Now with media attention and the Internet, more and more people are learning about transsexuals. And maybe now, some parents suspect their child is a transsexual; my heart goes out to them if they do. At least today there are some interceptive procedures such as blocking natural hormone production, which gives a child more time to develop without going through puberty. If the child is truly transsexual, he can be spared the agony of living with a totally alien body and having to reverse the effects of the natural hormones.

The umbrella term is transgender, which means any type of gender-crossing such as transvestism, cross-dressing, intersexuality and transsexuality. The term transsexual is generally limited to a person who desires to have sex change surgery. We were corrected many times by Angie, who insisted she was not to be called transgender, she was transsexual. We thought we were being politically correct by using transgender. We thought wrong, as in so many aspects of this entire experience.

I was simply appalled. Why? What had caused this? Couldn't we fix it? Surgery seemed an impossible option. How could anyone trust any surgeon to change their genitals? What if it was botched and he couldn't urinate? The cost had to be $50,000 to $100,000, and certainly was not covered by insurance. No, no, no, I insisted, this simply could not be.

Robert, on the other hand, was quite calm. He located a gender therapist at Westchester Medical Center in White Plains, New York. Donna Festa is the Gateway program coordinator who agreed to meet with us. My hope was that we could get to the bottom of this problem and correct it with therapy. Something must have caused this. Can a child truly have the wrong genitals? I simply could not believe it.

William met with Donna for about half an hour and then Donna called us in. "Angie and I have been chatting, and my job is to help her through this long process called transition."

Why was Donna calling him Angie? I thought we were here to explore the possibility that he was a transsexual, not to suddenly start calling him a girl's name and referring to him as "she." Donna had just met him. How did she know he was a girl?

"Now, this is very important, I can tell by the looks on your faces that you are confused. You came here with a boy and I'm calling him a girl. It's OK for you to be skeptical. You do not have to accept that Will is a girl. It is Angie's responsibility to convince you that she is a girl. She has a very long, difficult journey ahead, in which she must explore her life, and if she does everything she is supposed to do and if she follows the Standards of Care, then her actions will prove that surgery is necessary. This program is very difficult. She must prove to you that this is right for her. You do not have to just accept it."

Every word that Donna said made sense. I began to understand that there is no way to prove if a person is truly male or female. It is a matter of what their brain is telling them, and sometimes the brain gets signals mixed up. "I have lots of reading material for you, so don't try to remember all of this. But it seems," she explained, "that biological gender is actually a complex relationship of genetic, hormonal, morphological, chromosomal, gonadal, biochemical and anatomical determinates that impact the physiology of the body and the sexual differentiation of the brain. And to further complicate matters, there is not a test for gender; it can only be determined by an autopsy at death."

"Well, isn't that just absurd," I thought. But I began to understand that what was most important was that a person lives a life that is true to their feelings. If a person truly feels and believes they are the opposite gender, if the gender dysphoria has led to hatred of the genitals and the need for sexual reassignment, then according to the standards of care—the person is a transsexual. And with that diagnosis, no therapy can change those feelings

I understood every word she said—it made sense, but I definitely could not accept it.

The Standards of Care program is designed by the Harry Benjamin International Gender Dysphoria Association. Dr. Benjamin was an endocrinologist who pioneered treatment of transsexuals beginning in the 1950s. The program is designed for a person to systematically assume the role of the opposite gender. By exploring life as the opposite gender, they will prove to themselves and to others their true selves. They can turn back at any time. Even after they begin taking hormones, they can change their mind. The doctors also have to agree, and the surgeon who accepts them can refuse to operate if they feel it is not right, even up to the day before surgery.

With that meeting, we were set on a most difficult path that has taken us to the far corners of human understanding and potential. This was a journey that we reluctantly agreed to begin. My prayers, thoughts and sympathies are with any family that is about to undertake this journey. Please hang on tight for the rollercoaster ride of your life.

# Chapter 9
# I've been Ninja'd

"I'll be twenty when I graduate from high school. I can't do that. Homeschooling put me two years behind. My friends are laughing at me. I'm eighteen now, I should be graduating."

I had feared for years that we would have these repercussions. "Would you like to start college early?"

"What do you mean?"

"Why don't we go to the community college and talk to them about starting early? You're not required to graduate. You can get a GED."

"What's that?"

"It's a test you take instead of graduating. Then you can go to college. Do you want to go to college?"

"I hate high school. What do I have to do?"

We met with the counselor at Ulster Community College. Will withdrew from high school and passed the GED. He took placement tests for English and math, in which he placed at college level. Life was changing.

At the community college, Will began to feel more confident and happy with himself. I kept looking for signs that he didn't need to be a female. One day I saw a friend of his wearing a kilt and suggested since he was part Scottish that he might like to get his kilt.

"No, Mom. He's a guy, I'm not a guy. I am a girl!"

I was having more and more difficulty dealing with his desire to be a girl. I could not call him Angie. His friends called him Ange, so he suggested I try that. Ange was easier for me. So I began calling him Ange. One day he said that since the name was such a problem for me, maybe he would use the name that I had chosen for him if he had been born a girl.

"Jade would have been your name. Do you like Jade? Maybe I could call you that."

"Jade, yeah, I like that. You were going to name me Jade? That's neat."

So I started calling him Jade and kept trying to say "she." We went to the mall and bought a Jade ring for her to celebrate her new name.

Two months later, she told me that there was a porn star named Jade, so she was going to name herself Angie after all. I was disappointed, but understood, and I began calling her Angie. Still, I was hoping that she would change her mind about the surgery. Almost daily I watched for signs that she was not following the program.

I talked with her about hair, nails, makeup, and all of the maintenance that women require. I thought if she saw the aisle of feminine care products in the drug store—even transsexuals have vaginal issues, require lubrication, get infection—she would realize that being a woman is very difficult and not worth all the trouble.

It was to no avail; nothing deterred her or even bothered her. She started wearing makeup, painting her nails and letting her hair grow. Occasionally she went to the mall in a skirt. She was beginning her transition, with or without my support.

It was during this time that I started refusing to do her laundry. When I first discovered the girl's underwear a few years earlier, I just thought it was a teenage fetish. But then there were thongs and bikinis, bras and sexy lingerie. I couldn't stand touching it. I wanted him to stop wearing women's underwear.

We were visiting with friends who had teenagers and they were talking about the chores their kids did. "I got so tired of asking them to gather their dirty clothes," Cathy began. "I finally said, "OK guys this is it. Gather in the laundry room for a lesson and then you are on your own. If you don't have clean clothes, that's your problem."

So a few days later I called Angie into the laundry room, explained the way the machines work and advised that she would be leaving home soon and needed to know how to do laundry. I guess that wasn't so bad. She learned to do her own and she probably liked that better anyway. It actually worked out well. I don't know why I had been doing a teenager's laundry. It was time to start learning to be independent.

She was doing well in college. Every day she took the bus near our home in Highland to New Paltz, and then caught a bus to Ulster Community College. But she spent all of her free time in her room. She had no outside activities. In high school she had been on the track team, had been involved in drama and loved paint ball and rollerblading. Now all she did was go to school and hang out in her room.

In desperation, I hatched a plan to get her out of the house and out on her own so she could explore this new life without me hovering over her or interfering.

"Angie, this is a paper for college that you need to sign."

"OK." And with that she signed her application to SUNY Cobleskill, a four-year school in the Catskill Mountains of New York. Three months later we went on a little field trip to Cobleskill.

"So, what do you think of this campus?" Robert was very excited. He had attended Cobleskill before he went to Oregon State University. We had chosen it because it had a two-year program in culinary arts and Angie had said many times that she wanted to be a chef.

"This is really neat, but why are we here?" She had walked through the whole campus and was standing in a dorm room.

"Remember that form you signed a few months ago for college?"

"No, but whatever."

"You've been accepted here for the fall—but it's your decision. You only have to come if you really want to."

"You mean I can go to a real college, even with a GED? I didn't know I could go anywhere except the community college."

"I wasn't sure you could transfer either; that's why we didn't mention anything to you earlier. But you've been accepted to Cobleskill into the Culinary Arts Program to be a chef."

"A chef? What if I don't want to be a chef?"

"We'll talk to the registrar and see if you can change to another program. I don't think it'll be a problem. The important thing is that you're accepted and you can decide if you want to come."

"I've been Ninja'd. That was a sneaky trick—but I like it. Neat. I never thought I could go to a real college. Wow! I can leave home. Wow!"

# Chapter 10
# You want to fix me?

I didn't want to believe that he would actually follow the entire transition and become a female. I felt that William was committing suicide. One day we were having a session with Donna, the gender therapist, and I began pleading with him not to go through with it. "Remember our martial arts training, the yin and yang, the male and female. All of us have masculine and feminine qualities. What you are proposing is to destroy your masculine. Can't you just be gender-neutral, dress up as a female sometimes and not destroy Will? Why do you have to have surgery? I just don't understand."

Angie and Donna both looked at me as if I were delusional. And maybe I did sound desperate, which I was. I was pleading for the life of my child. I felt that she was trying to destroy any traces of William, the dear child I had known for seventeen years.

"You don't have to understand, Mom. You just have to accept this. I am a girl. I was born a girl and have known it for a very long time. I can't live with this body. I can't even look at myself in the mirror. Do you know that I wanted to commit suicide last year, or worse, to cut all that stuff off? The only thing that kept me from mutilating myself is that they need all that stuff to make my new body, my vagina, Mom. I'm going to have a vagina. I am a girl."

But where was my son? If he was truly a girl, how did I not know it? How had I not noticed anything before? Wouldn't I have suspected something? How could he just think that he could have surgery, destroy the boy I knew and become a totally different person—a girl named Angela? How could he hate himself so much and think that he could be happy living as a girl?

"Mom, why can't you just accept this?"

"I feel the same way I would feel if you told me that you could jump off a building and fly. I feel that if I accept this and support you, I'm allowing you to commit suicide. I don't want to lose my son. I don't know this girl, Angie, that you say you are. You are a stranger to me."

"What do I need to do to convince you, Mom?"

"I don't think I can accept this."

"Then you will not only lose a son, you will lose a daughter."

"I don't want to lose you, Angie. I am trying to understand and I really want to love you. I know it must just feel horrible to think that you are really a girl and to hate your body so much. That part scares me, and I really think that I feel your pain. It's just that you are so sure that this is the right thing to do, but I don't know how to accept it. It's very, very difficult to see you as Angie instead of Will."

"Angie," began Donna. "It's important that you understand that other people, including your parents, feel they have been blindsided. You feel inside that you must express yourself, but they only see the old person you've always been. They will need lots of time, maybe years, to accept this change. Some parents never accept it, and many totally reject their children. Give your parents some time. Please try to think about how it feels to them."

"I want my parents to accept the real me, not someone that they thought I was."

I took William to the monthly group sessions with other transsexuals. Sitting in the waiting room and watching the members of the group file in was a lesson in trying to keep a straight face, while wanting to gasp and scream, "My son is nothing like these people!" The group members were all middle-aged men dressing like fourteen-year-old girls. Didn't they know how ridiculous they looked? Why couldn't Will see that he wasn't like them? Why did he want to look like them?

They all wore way too much makeup. They had on short skirts. Some looked like they could be football players; they had broad shoulders and were over six feet tall. What was going on in their minds? Would they really go through with surgery, or was this just a passing thing?

My gut reaction was to laugh. But, with my own son there dressing and looking so similar, what I felt next was a deep sadness. Despite their light banter and silly clothes, I could feel the turmoil down deep. I tried to imagine how they had struggled for years. I had read enough by that time to know that most transsexuals realized from the time they were children that they were in the wrong body. I had learned that many of them overcompensated and tried to suppress it by becoming macho—soldiers, policemen. Many of them wanted to have surgery very young, but their families rejected them or they knew it was impossible to afford. Many began the transition only when the other option was suicide. A searing, gaping hole pierced my heart. While William attended the meetings, I walked the halls weeping openly.

Leaving the meeting one night, Will said, "I'm not like them."

I wanted to jump up and down, shout to the heavens, "Thank you, God. He doesn't want to be a girl." Rob was right; going through this transition would show him that he was not a girl, I felt so relieved that now he was beginning to see. I was so glad that we were struggling through this long difficult process together, and now maybe we could get the therapy he needed to accept himself.

Walking back to the car, I felt my shoulders relaxing; I took a deep breath and slowly exhaled. "I'm so glad, Will.

We'll do everything we can to find out what's going on and try to fix it."

He turned to me abruptly with a quizzical look. "Fix it? You want to fix me the way they try to fix homosexuals. There's nothing that can fix me, except surgery. You totally misunderstood what I said. You heard what you wanted to hear, not what I was trying to tell you. I'm not like them 'cause they're all so old. They all said that they wanted to go through this many years ago at my age. They didn't do it then, and now it's harder 'cause they're so old. No, I'm not like them. I'm doing this now! I wish I had done it years ago."

# Chapter 11
# Please don't do this

During the first two years of the transition, I totally avoided discussing my children with anyone. We couldn't tell anyone about the transition, because it was Angie's personal journey and it was her responsibility to tell other people when she was ready. So, I simply changed the subject if anyone started discussing their children or asked me if I had children. I honestly didn't know what to say. Should I say, "I have two daughters and a he/she? I used to have a son, but now he's"—oh God, I didn't know what he was or what he was to become. I just wanted it to all go away and let me have my son back.

During the first year of the transition, he would occasionally wear a skirt or put on some makeup. He was not rushing into living full-time as a female. I hoped that meant that he was thinking of changing his mind. When I saw him dressed in jeans with no makeup, I secretly told myself, "He won't go through with it. It will pass soon and we'll be back to normal."

But then I would think to myself, "Back to 'normal?' Really now, is that what you want? He was so depressed for the last few years, he wanted to commit suicide. Why, why, why? Isn't there another solution? Can't we fix this?"

We were walking through the Poughkeepsie Galleria one day. He had on a short skirt, heels and a blouse. His hair was about chin length, a really bad, shaggy hairdo. His eye shadow was bright blue with heavy black eye liner. Each person who passed stared at him and either poked their friend or shook their head in disbelief. He was obviously a boy dressed up as a girl. I was embarrassed for him.

I wanted to hug him and say, "I'm so sorry you have to go through this. Do you really think that it will be worth it? Do you think that you will really pass as a girl? Right now you just look so bad, so out of place and confused."

He never seemed to mind how he looked. I guess when he looked in the mirror; he saw who he was becoming. He had a strange self-confidence that defied my understanding. He was happy with himself. He was pacing himself, getting ready for the day when he would begin to live full-time as a female.

Unfortunately for me, that day was the day we took him to SUNY Cobleskill to live in the men's dorm. "Why today?" I kept asking myself. I had talked with him for several weeks about giving himself time to adjust to the college and to slowly begin dressing up. To let it be a gradual change, after he got to know some people and could explain to them what he was doing.

But no, as he explained to me, it was better to start off from the first day living as a female. Donna had written a letter to the school informing them that he was a transsexual going through transition, and she had requested a private room. She said, "Now, of course, you understand they will not give you a private room, but we'll request it anyway."

We drove in silence. I kept sneaking a peek at him in the back seat, trying to imagine the reactions from the other students. I mean, seriously, he was checking into the men's dorm—a boy who was dressed up like a girl, water balloon bra and all. I felt that searing pain through my chest. I wished I could protect him from the difficulties that lay ahead. I was almost beginning to accept that he was going through with this, and I knew he was beginning one of the most difficult journeys that a human can take. I was willing to tag along, but I sure wished he didn't have to go through with it.

He checked in, acting like everything was normal. I watched the shocked looks, wide eyes and nervous smiles.

If I could have traded places with him, I would have stepped in.

And then we had to meet his roommate and his father. Will and his roommate began chatting easily about gaming, computers, classes and things they wanted to do with the room. The young man didn't seem to notice or just didn't care that Will was dressed as a girl. They found lots of common ground immediately. Rob was chatting with the roommate's father. Suddenly, in the middle of the room, Will took off his sweater and stood there with a skintight T-shirt clinging to his water balloon bra.

I gasped and ran from the room. Hiding in the car, I just wanted to die. I couldn't take any more of this. It was more than I could live through. "Stop this, stop this, and please don't do this. Oh God, stop the world, I want to get off."

Eventually Rob and Will found me, and Will said he would wait until I left to dress up again. "Please, Mom, I had to dress from the first day. It just has to be this way. I'm sorry this bothers you, but this is my life and it's going to be this way from now on. Come on with us, I have to get my ID and meal card. Then you can just go back home and leave me to live my life."

I was ravaged by guilt. I wished I could be stronger and more supportive for him. I loved him dearly and my heart was breaking from grief.

# Chapter 12
## She could be murdered!

Most of the two years after Angie started Cobleskill is a blur to me. I was terrified that she would be attacked, beaten up, raped or killed. She reported that she was harassed and threatened many times.

"Mom, is Dad there?"

"No, he was called out on an emergency. What's wrong? What time is it?"

"It's about five in the morning. I'm at the police station in Cobleskill."

Suddenly wide awake, I screamed, "Oh, God, what's wrong?"

"This guy has been bothering me a lot. He's been banging on my door at all hours of the night, calling me a fag. He and his friends are always tripping me in the hall. So I got really tired of it. I rigged up my door so that when he banged on it, it would fly open and I could catch him. So anyway, we're both here at the police station."

"Are you hurt? Is he hurt? Are you in trouble? What do we need to do?"

"No, nobody's hurt. He just got really pissed when he fell into my room and we started screaming and the whole floor woke up and we both got in trouble. The police came."

"So what do we need to do? Dad and I will be there in a few hours. You want us to come, don't you?"

"No. No. Don't come. I have to handle this alone. I just wanted to talk."

I read every news item ever written about transsexuals who were murdered or beaten. I was in a constant state of anxiety. She was at a conservative, agricultural school. "Did we send her to her death?" I kept asking myself. I felt her life was in constant danger.

But despite the social difficulties at Cobleskill, Angie loved school. She was studying video editing and had a 3.8 GPA. She filmed two documentaries about her life as a transsexual which later won awards. She made many friends. After only two weeks at school, she had been moved to a private room, and eventually onto the girls' floor, although she was expected to use the boys' bath. We let her live her life and had very little contact with her.

As the end of the second school year approached, we received a letter from the school inviting us to the awards banquet. "Angie is getting an award, we need to be there." Robert glared at me. "We are going. You'll just have to find a way to keep yourself calm and deal with this."

We had not met any of her friends, teachers or the counselor she saw regularly. "I'm sure they all think we are horrible, horrible parents who have rejected her and don't love her. You read that article she wrote for the school newspaper. Do you think they feel we are terrible parents?"

"Everybody knows that kids hate their parents," Rob said. "I think you worry too much about what other people think. How do you know when a teenager is lying? When they're talking, that's how. These people probably know that all young kids exaggerate the problems they have with their parents. You know who you really need to worry about? The kids who never say anything, the ones who never talk about their home life and the problems. They are probably the ones whose parents are abusive. The fact that she's talking about us and yes, telling everybody what a horrible mother you are, is probably a good thing. Someday she'll forgive us. Well, I hope so anyway."

I could barely drag myself to the auditorium.

"Here they are! Mom, Dad over here, I want you to meet my advisor, my teachers and all my friends."

She was wearing a miniskirt, spiked heels, and her well-worn red fishnet top with a red spaghetti strap camisole. Her makeup was applied in moderation, not to much. I saw my daughter for the first time. She was on her home turf. She was happy. She was introducing us to her friends and her teachers. She was laughing and talking comfortably as if everything was absolutely normal.

"And look what Mom brought me. Look, look, isn't she just the cutest little purple Care Bear you've ever seen. Mom knows I love Care Bears. Last year for Easter she gave me a pink Care Bear, and of course, you've seen Brave Heart Lion. He's my favorite."

I wanted to savor the moment. She was so comfortable with herself and her surroundings. Her friends seemed to genuinely care for her. Her teachers praised her hard work and great grades. This was my daughter, and I felt genuine love toward her for the first time.

We walked into the auditorium for the service to begin, and my heart sank. I saw that she would have to walk up the stairs to the stage, accept her award and then walk down the stairs on the other side. How much experience did she have walking in high heels? My palms were sweating. I was taking deep breaths and praying.

"And the award for the Highest GPA for Communications Majors—"

I held my breath, ground my teeth and gripped the leather seat. She sashayed down the aisle, bounced lightly up the stairs, accepted her award to thunderous applause, took the stairs two at a time and was grinning at me before I could even exhale.

# Chapter 13
# I'm not the only sad one in the family

She was continuing the program set up by the gender specialist. She was living full-time as a female and had begun to tell all of her former friends and our families about her life. Almost everyone was accepting and supportive. Many family members and some of our close friends contacted her and offered to meet with her or talk with her anytime she needed to talk. They all said they couldn't imagine how we could go through with what we were doing. A few acquaintances were not supportive; some even said that they simply would not allow it, that they would have kicked him out of the house and out of their lives.

Sometimes I would see William in Angie's actions or mannerisms. It was always just a fleeting moment. He always seemed like a shadow or ghost—part of Angie, but only in the background. I had difficulty sleeping. I began to have a recurring nightmare that I had gone to the daycare center to get Will and he wasn't there. He had gotten lost and they couldn't find him. Many nights I woke up crying, grieving the loss of my son. I was depressed and withdrawn. I didn't keep in touch with our other daughters or the grandchildren.

Anyone who has a special-needs child knows that the siblings suffer from neglect, and I had been guilty of neglecting them for many years. Will had so many problems from birth that I had probably neglected our older girls from that moment on.

We were told many times by our daughters that we babied Will and did too much for him. They were right. We did, but we didn't feel we had much choice. We were trying to let him be independent, but he had so much going against him.

And now we had Angie who, like most transsexuals in their early years of transition, was much like a fourteen-year-old girl. I was nearly sixty, ready to retire, too old to have a teenager. My health suffered. I developed an ulcer and several other medical problems. I cried all the time and was just plain miserable.

Concerned for my health, Robert suggested I spend some time in North Carolina with my family. I jumped at the chance to be away from New York. Before he could change his mind, I was making a mental list of the CDs I would need for a two-day trip. "Alison Krause, Beethoven, Billy Ray Cyrus, Bocelli, CCR, Carmina Burana, Carrie Underwood, Carreras, yep, yep, that one, and that too, and Zorba the Greek."

I had the Nissan loaded and was speedin' down I-81 through Pennsylvania, heading for I-64 which would take me into Richmond, then down I-95 to home. I was savoring the taste of chicken and pastry, fried okra, barbeque, turnip greens, eggs and grits—and that was just from eating breakfast, lunch and supper at Cracker Barrel. I was "fuller 'an a tick" by the time I hit the Mason-Dixon line. Of course, that didn't keep me from stopping for barbeque at Smithfield and at another Cracker Barrel for a pecan bar, the extra large one.

As I crossed the state line into North Carolina, James Taylor—whose father was dean of the medical school when I was at Chapel Hill—was blasting: "In my mind I'm goin' to Carolina." With my Cracker Barrel Front Porch Friends' card and my UNC-Chapel Hill Alumni Visa card, I was like a drunken fool on a bender. I was singing along to Zorba the Greek as I happily drove south on Highway 17, heading to the beach. "Let it grow, let it last. Think about the story of the butterfly. The but...ter...fly...Oh, Angie, my little butterfly." I had to pull off the road and have a good cry before I could continue.

⊰⊱

I spent the late fall and winter of 2006 in North Carolina with my family. I wasn't ready to tell my parents about Angie, but our time together was well-spent. I woke up every morning with the sun coming up over the Intracoastal Waterway and watched the sunset over the bay. It was an ideal retreat. I played my violin, took long walks on the beach and ate enough barbeque, shrimp and okra to gain a little weight.

Mama is the best cook in the South and I was hungry for her fried okra. That okra created the biggest fights I had with my sisters—who would get the most okra. We would steal it off each other's plates. One time I called my sister Ruby Ann and told her she couldn't come for supper 'cause Mama had one of her spells and was laid up—I lied. I just wanted to eat all the okra, and that was when I was a grown woman. We were downright vicious.

Mama never let me cook when I was growing up. She caught me stirring the giblet gravy with my pellet gun once. That was all it took: "No tomboys allowed in the kitchen." My favorite cake was my grandmother's pound cake so I asked Grandmother if she would give me her recipe. "Do how? Give you my recipe? And have you ruin my cake. Not in my lifetime, chil'." Finally when I was grown she gave it to me, so I set out to make Crystal's birthday cake. Two dozen eggs and about ten pounds of flour later, I told Crystal that birthday cakes are optional. For her fourth birthday, she made it herself and did better than I did. She was precocious and could read by the time she was four. "If you can read, you can cook," I told her.

So I was visiting my parents that fall of 2006 and spending lots of time on the beach. One day I was walking through the surf, kicking the water, running from the waves. It was early morning after a storm. I was looking for sand dollars and I saw tiny footprints. It was barely daybreak; there was no one else on the beach. I followed the small child's footprints all along the point at Oak Island.

"William, are you here? Where are you?" Will was splashing in the surf. "Catch the wave, Will. Bring your boogie board over here; there are lots of big waves."

"Watch me, Mom." He flopped on the board and began to paddle out.

"Not too far, Will. The waves can get pretty big." I shielded my eyes to try to get a better glimpse of him. He kept going farther and farther out into the waves. "Will, come back. That's too far."

"No, Mom. I'm OK. I know what I'm doing." He turned toward me and waved slowly. He had a crooked, sinister grin. He turned away, rolled over into the water and started swimming out to sea. "Bye, Mom. Why couldn't you just accept me? Now you'll lose me. Bye, Mom," he shouted.

"No. No. Come back. Somebody help me!" I screamed. "He'll drown. He's swimming out to sea, he'll die. Help me. Please don't let him die."

In a panic, I awoke with a start. How could this be happening? Why, why, why?

I needed to get away, so I called my cousin Brian, the closest I had to a brother. "Hey, how you doin'? Can I come to the homeplace? I haven't seen you in years."

I sped northwest along NC 87 toward Tar Heel but on the way I had to stop at Melvin's in Elizabethtown for the best Carolina burger: hand shaped Angus burger with finely chopped coleslaw, chili, onions and mustard—can't beat their burgers. Then I stopped in Dublin to buy some peanuts for Robert, before continuing to the little town—well, cross roads. There's not much of a town in Tar Heel, population 70.

The Nissan slowed to a crawl as I bumped over the plank bridge crossing the dried creek bed. Shaggy brown heads rose from the grass, turned toward the car, and then resumed cud chewing. The pines stood as sentinels along both sides of the quarter mile drive. A smoky, maple scent pervaded the air.

Brian said he'd probably be out on the tractor, and no one else lived there, so I just strolled across the sand-choked grass. The paper shell pecans cracked underfoot. Magnolia blossoms lay rotting beneath the trees. I took a long, deep breath.

I raced up the wooden front steps. Breathing heavily, I leaned against one of the columns on the wide front porch. The paint-chipped rocking chairs sat like old men trying to make sense out of their remaining days.

With both hands, I grasped the brass door handle. "Uhh," I groaned. The door swung open and clunked into the cast-iron Scotty dog, pushing him into the dark paneling of the center hall colonial. The door slammed shut with a "vaboomk" that echoed down the empty hallway. I sprinted down the wood plank floor. "I'm home. I'm home." The memories flooded back. This is my favorite place. This is where I spent every summer and every vacation. This is the homeplace. At that moment I was bombarded by memories.

I imagined the familiar sounds of my childhood, of Hattie's high-pitched voice screeching orders. "You good fo' nothin' boy. You git yo' lazy black backside out and slop them hawgs."

I grasped the porcelain handle and pushed the white door into the kitchen, remembering the steamy heaven. I longed to smell the chicken and pastry, fried okra, vinegar and collard greens, creamed corn, cinnamon rolls, and pecan pie. I longed too for Hattie's hugs and to hear her familiar singsong voice. Just to hear her say again, "Lawsy mercy, chil'. My, how you growed! Why, if you ain't the spit-tin' image of yo' Aint May. Come give yo' Hattie a hug."

I could imagine those great chestnut arms flung straight out, then crushing me into her soft bosom of starched cotton, sweat and jasmine. I felt surrounded by love and good memories.

Standing in the empty house, memories flashed back to me vividly. It was a Christmas vacation visit while I was in college. My first question was always, "How's Mama?" That Christmas, Hattie sighed heavily and dabbed her eyes with her apron.

"Oh, honey," she said. "I think yo' mama done got her weakness again so they's coming for her to rest. Should be he-ah any minute. Don't you upset yo' Mama. You he-ah?"

"I'll be good. I promise. I better say hello to Aunt Ida."

"Well, she's takin' tea now. You can join her in the par-lor."

I balanced the tea cup and saucer on my plaid wool skirt. I was trying to act like a grown up. I lifted the cup half-way to my lips, then replaced it. "Aunt Ida," I began tenta-tively. "Why does Mama have these nervous breakdowns? And what is a nervous breakdown?"

"That's just a silly term some doctor made up, not a real sickness. In your mama's case, I think it's her sadness." The grandfather clock ticked louder and louder as the silence between us grew. After dabbing her eyes with her embroi-dered handkerchief, Aunt Ida adjusted the silver brooch on her Edwardian style blouse. She uncrossed her ankles, then crossed them again as she shifted in the Victorian arm chair. She patted the neat silver bun at the nape of her neck. "You know that her mother died when she was sev-en. That's when she came to live with us. She never talked about it—just went on like nothing happened. Sadness has a way of catching up with us later in life. It's like treading water your whole life, and then you just get so tired, you sink to the bottom. She just needs to rest awhile, then she'll be up and running again. She always recovers quickly."

Aunt Ida drummed her fingers lightly on the polished mahogany. She lowered her eyes and tightened her jaw. "My dear, you are not to upset your mother, understand? Don't start arguing with your father about who you should or should not marry."

I nodded obediently.

"Tomorrow afternoon is our DAR meeting; I expect you'll be joining me as usual. I need to review some notes. Will you excuse me?"

"Yes, ma'am." "Old suffer in silence," I thought. "The women of this family must have a history of just clamming up. Can't anything ever be out in the open? Can't we for once talk about something? Anything?"

I can still remember pacing the floor, waiting for Mama and Daddy. And then suddenly the cacophony of yelps and barks from Brian's pack of hounds broke the silence. The sturdy black Pontiac lumbered to a crawl by the side door. My chest tightened and I swallowed hard. The clock innocently clanged the seconds to our confrontation.

"Miss Rhonda May, they's he-ah."

"Thank you, Hattie," I whispered to the figure scurrying back down the hall. I squared my shoulders and stood stiffly by the fireplace with one hand cradled in the other. I held my chin high and swore that I would not get into an argument with Daddy. I clenched my teeth tighter as my mother's giddy twitter approached.

With blue-white arms flailing like flags warning of imminent danger, Mama led Daddy into the room. She reminded me of a rodeo clown bobbing and swaying to divert the attention of the bull from the fallen cowboy. I knew this heroic gesture would take any remaining strength from this sad creature who spent a good deal of time curled into her nervous breakdown barrel, while life butted it about.

I fought back tears, the lump in my throat threatening to choke me. I hugged Mama and wiped the tears from her chalk-white face and pushed the straggles of brown hair out of her sad, questioning eyes.

Daddy strolled into the room twirling his brown fedora. "You've probably heard that your mother is ill again. I expect that you will not upset her like you usually do. And how is school?"

"Fine, sir."

"Has Chapel Hill rendered a fine professional for you to marry?"

I felt the hot flush rise in my cheeks. "I'm not sure that I will find one, sir."

Apparently sensing danger, Mama's white arm-flags flailed their warning. So I quickly added, "but...but I'm sure I will, sir, maybe the medical student I've been dating."

"Your mother needs to rest for the remainder of the day. You can visit with her in the morning. Hattie, please take Mother to her room."

Aunt Ida told me that I was like Mama. "She was such a lively young girl. A lot like you." I wondered if I would end up like her, having those nervous breakdowns. I lingered in the front hall listening to the whir of the gas heater. I heard the china plates scrape together, then thud onto the table-cloth. The scent of silver polish drifted through the air. The crystal tinkled sweetly.

Hattie's full voice sank into a low dirge. "Little orphan Annie come to our house to stay. She washed the cups and saucers and swept the crumbs away." The plaintive cry of a mourning dove accompanied Hattie's portentous chant. Tears welled up in my eyes.

I couldn't wait till morning, so I tiptoed down the hall and peeked into the room where Mama lay. I was drawn to the chalky face surrounded by white lace pillows. I tiptoed over the blue braided rug to the mahogany four poster bed. "Mama," I whispered. The vacant eyes slowly turned toward me.

"Aunt May?"

"No, Mama. It's me, Rhonda May." I buried my face in the coverlet and stroked the sad face. "Oh, Mama, be strong for me. I need you."

"I want you to have this, Rhonda May. It's my diamond; I've been saving it for you, since it's your birthstone."

"No, Mama. You can't give your jewelry away. I'll keep it for awhile and then give it back when you feel better." She smiled faintly and nodded like an obedient child. I arranged the pillows, folded her hands together, and touched her lightly on her cheek. "There is no God. He'd never allow this to happen to you." I kissed her lightly, wiped the tears from her cheeks and tiptoed out of the room.

The soft, mellow gas lights cast eerie shadows down the long hallway. That night I sat for hours cross-legged in front of the gas heater, watching the flames leap across the porcelain grates. I thought of the women in my family. How sadness had consumed so many of them. I wondered if that would also be my fate. Holding my hand up with fingers fanned out, I watched the diamond flicker bits of light. "Are we just bits of charcoal mined out of the deep troubled abyss of our family? Occasionally, under the right light, we shine briefly, and then die." I wrapped my arms around my knees, hugged them, and slowly rocked back and forth.

I jumped suddenly. I held my breath. "Don't move, she'll get you," I whispered. I stared at the window. The full moon had reached the arc of the high window. Distorted by the imperfections of the ancient glass, it resembled a skull. The stark tree branches scratched on the frosted panes.

"Who...who...whooo."

A little scream escaped from my clenched teeth. "Just an owl, you ass," I hissed under my breath. I shook all over. The skeletal fingers of moonlight slithered throughout the room, groping the furniture and entombing me in cavernous shadow. I was riveted to the window. "I wonder if she can see me. I won't move. I won't blink. I won't even breathe."

Silhouetted in the window, the lone figure stood gazing out. One hand rested on the sill, the other yanked at the long flowing white gown. She grabbed her waist-length dark hair, twisting it around her head, then letting it fall over her face and shoulders. She tried to turn the latch on the window. She pounded the sill with both hands. But there was no sound. She abruptly stood still. She cocked her head slightly to one side. Suddenly she turned from the window and peered straight at me.

My heart was pounding. I felt icy but began to perspire. The hair stood up on the back of my neck. I tried to hold my breath but it kept forcing its way out in spasmodic heaves. A chill ran up my spine and spread to my fingertips. I squeezed my eyes shut.

"You're being really stupid," I said loudly. Without looking at the window again, I yanked my chenille housecoat off the hook, jammed my arms into it and padded barefoot down the hall. I heard Aunt Ida's voice and Mama's so I tentatively pushed the door open.

"Mama, I'm so glad you're all right. I was so worried about you. I just scared myself nearly to death. I thought I saw a ghost. I was terrified."

I looked from my mother to my aunt, who were locked in a conspirators' gaze. Aunt Ida coughed nervously. "Now dear, don't upset yourself. This house is old. There are so many stories. You can't believe all that stuff. Just forget about it. I certainly wouldn't know about any ghosts. You just had a bad dream," she said with a huff. She rose abruptly and left the room.

But the house was empty that day in 2006. Everyone was long gone except my cousin, Brian, the only one who still lives there.

I waited in Uncle Jim's library, running my fingers along the spines of ancient leather-bound volumes and looking at faded pictures of ancestors. Sadness seemed to be reflected through the years.

As I had predicted that Christmas so many years ago, I also had succumbed to the depression like the other women in my family. And I feared that my daughters would suffer the same fate. We tend to follow in the steps of our mothers, whether we learn it by observing them or whether it's genetic is hard to know. But it's important to know our history, to recognize the symptoms in ourselves and to seek help as soon as possible.

I found a copy of the diary of my ancestor, Aunt Elizabeth, which she kept from 1847 to 1866. It had been transcribed by Aunt Ida and we all had copies. The original has been microfilmed by the State Department of Archives and History and is on file there. I have read the diary so many times that my own copy is now dog-eared, with pages falling out. I always read it when my life is in turmoil. Reading her diary gives me courage to continue my battles.

It was Oct 27, 2006, so I turned to that date in history. *October 27, 1850. This day about 3 o'clock my darling son breathed his last. O merciful Father, lead me in the way I should go, do as Thou thinkest best with me but spare my soul...I have consigned five beloved children to the grave... But Gooderum my sixth is the most precious as he had grown to manhood...*

The screen door creaked and I looked up to see Brian, wiping his brow with his sleeve and holding his straw hat in his hand. "It's been a few years, Rhonda May. Good to see you. Let me get some iced tea and you can tell me when you're coming back home to live."

We talked for hours. Growing up together, he was my closest friend. "It's going to be hard to tell your mama, but you just got to do it. Nobody else can tell her. I'm certainly not going to say anything. No, ma'am. Get my head chewed off? Not on your life. So, how is Angie? When will we get to meet her? Is she as pretty as you? I bet she looks just like you when you were young."

It was nearing nightfall as I drove back to the quaint little fishing village on the Intracoastal Waterway where my granddaddy had been a charter member of the fishing club. I slid the Nissan quietly onto the sandy drive under the live oak tree and slipped unnoticed into my little cabin by the pier. "Not this trip. But I'll have to tell them soon. It's my responsibility. Oh Great Spirit, give me strength to fight my greatest enemy—myself."

# Chapter 14
# Teamwork

I hated going back to New York. Robert and I had bought property in North Carolina—actually, we bought Granddaddy's beach property complete with fishing hut—and we had planned to retire close to my parents and build a house. There was no hope of retiring any time soon. I simply did not know how I could tolerate New York winters any more or how I could deal with a teenage girl.

Returning to New York, I decided to return to work full-time, which I hadn't been able to do for many years. I've never had a career; the closest I came to a career was working as an accountant, which then led to an opportunity to take the Series 7 exam and become a stockbroker for Merrill Lynch. Unfortunately, since I was only a stockbroker for a few years, my career ended with the crash of October 19, 1987. By then, William needed me at home more than I needed to work.

So when I returned to New York in 2007, I took a job as a customer service representative for a large medical insurance company, a job that is extremely difficult, but somehow one at which I seem to excel. Through the years I must have developed patience, compassion and the ability to listen to irate customers.

Robert had worked for New York State for many years and ten years ago became an environmental engineer and emergency responder for the Department of Environmental Conservation. After twenty-five years of marriage, we had developed some financial security; we finally felt comfortable and were just beginning to look forward to retirement.

But then we had a new daughter who was planning to have major surgery, and suddenly our life felt like it was placed in a weird holding pattern. Rob was agonizing over whether we could ever retire. We constantly worried about Angie. We had not had a vacation, even a weekend together to relax for many years.

"I think for our anniversary we should do something special," he began. "I think we should go to Mohonk for a weekend."

I stared in disbelief. "You know we can't afford that, those rooms start at three or four hundred a night. How could we possibly do it?"

"I know, but if we end up paying for Angie's surgery, it's going to take everything we have and we'll never do anything for ourselves. We never have. We never even had a honeymoon; we've never had a vacation. We really deserve something. I've been saving all my money from working overtime and I've already paid for the rooms, the dogs are going to the kennel. Go pack your bags. We're leaving this afternoon."

I'm not a spontaneous person. Surprises usually upset me. But this time I just shook my head slowly and started packing. "A weekend at Mohonk, wow!"

It was like a dream. After dropping the dogs off at the kennel, we drove the few miles from our home in Highland through downtown New Paltz. "You've seen that tower up on the top of that mountain thousands of times," Rob said, pointing to the Shawangunk Mountains that we can see from our hometown. "We're going to Mohonk Mountain House for the weekend."

The house is actually a castle built in 1849 by the Smiley Brothers, a Quaker family that still owns it to this day. It's on the National Registry. Perched on top of a mountain by a blue sky lake, it has been a get-away for celebrities and the very wealthy ever since it was built. It's only a twenty-minute drive from our home, and I had always wanted to stay there but knew that it was impossible.

As our little Nissan grumbled up the mountain, I still could not believe I was going to one of my favorite places, not just for day hiking as we had done before, but to stay for two nights. We arrived at the heavily guarded gate.

"Lots of cars waiting. Wonder what's taking so long to get through the checkpoint," said Rob, who can be a little impatient sometimes. "Are those dogs? They're sniffing the cars. Are they checking for drugs? What the hell?"

"Maybe they're sniffing for bombs."

"Now Rhonda, why would they have bomb-sniffing dogs at a resort?"

We got through the gate finally and began our ascent to the house. We pulled off occasionally to take in the land-scape, the views of the mountains and the sky. We were in a totally foreign land, thousand of acres protected from de-velopment. Miles of hiking trails were built with little wooden gazebos lining the different outcroppings. Sharp cliffs gave way to thick foliage on the sides of the mountains.

Stepping out of the car and slowly wandering into the lobby, we were transported back in time. The entire house is furnished with antiques. Our room was one of the Victorian rooms with a fireplace and marble bath fixtures. I walked out onto the balcony overlooking the lake. "You picked a great room. I love the view."

We wandered around the house for hours after we enjoyed the afternoon tea. Rob has never met a stranger, so he was chatting with one of the employees who was building a fire in one of the many fireplaces. "We're here for our anniversary. We've always wanted to stay. Have you worked here long?"

I wandered off to enjoy the library, the bird feeder that is inside the window and the many antiques and artworks throughout the house. The center staircase of spindled, highly polished wood, winds round and round up to the top floor. As I was gazing all the way to the top, I caught a glimpse of a young woman with curly brown hair, taking the stairs two at a time. She was followed closely by two men in dark suits. "That's weird."

Rob found me later rocking on the wide porch which travels the length of the house. "It's really good to get away, isn't it? This is where you come to get away from the world."

And we were on top of the world. As I gazed over many miles, I let the world fade away. I truly had stopped the world and gotten off. I was away from everything. I took a deep breath and thanked the heavens for just one weekend of freedom together, far from the worries of home.

I was thankful that Rob can act on the spur of the moment and not think too much about the practical matters that bog us down. I was thankful that we are very different and can balance each other. If it had been up to me, I never would have allowed this luxury. This was pure heaven.

We were wandering around the house when I noticed a woman about my age, deep in thought, strolling down the hall. Behind her about ten feet were two men in dark suits. She passed us, nodded and continued down the hall.

"Well I guess that explains the bomb-sniffing dogs." Rob grinned.

Hillary must have needed a break from her presidential campaigning and was enjoying a rest at Mohonk.

"I guess that also explains why I couldn't get the tower room for you. I tried to reserve that one, but they said it was taken, so I had to get a Victorian room."

"You are such a liar. I'm not gullible enough to believe you would have gotten the tower room. So don't even go there. I love it here. I'm in another world. It's a true escape. Thank you for a great surprise."

We returned to our room to dress for dinner. On the bed was a gift from the house that said, "Happy Anniversary."

"That guy I was talking to must have gone right over to the front desk and told them it's our anniversary. Don't that beat all."

# Chapter 15
# Building walls

"Rhonda, what in the hell are you doin'?"

Panting and wheezing, I chucked another rock, "Uhhh. I'm movin' these rocks. If life gives you rocks, you make a rock garden."

"You got all these out of the woods? Were you doin' this the whole time I was gone?"

"Yeah, the whole week." I heaved another boulder.

"Are you out of your mind? There's thousands of huge rocks here. You tryin' to kill yourself?"

Slumping, I dropped my head into my hands. "I'm just so angry. Angry at God. I'm angry at William, or Angie or whoever that is. I just want to scream sometimes. I can't stand it. Why does he have to do this? Why is she so happy and I'm so miserable? I just want to shake her or punch her. I would love to spar with her. We'd put on our boxing gloves and punch and kick. Just like the good ole days when we were in Taekwondo. I just have to do something, I have so much anxiety that I just need to keep moving."

"There are martial arts schools here. Why don't you start training again? You're a black belt."

"Now who's crazy? I'm too old; I was forty-five then, now I'm fifty-eight. I'm so old and tired. I would love to just punch someone. I loved sparring."

"Yeah, I know. You loved it too much. Remember when you were at nationals and I thought you had gotten a broken nose? I was so mad at you. But I couldn't talk you out of it. How many trophies and medals did you and Will get?"

"Lots and lots. Did you hear what Billy said when he was here with Ally a few weeks ago? He came tiptoeing up to me and said 'Nana, what are all those trophies for?' I started telling him about Taekwondo and Ally broke in, 'Billy, your nana is Kung Fu Panda!' I wish you could have seen him. His eyebrows shot up, he opened his eyes wide and his mouth dropped open. It was so cute. But I'm not Kung Fu Panda anymore. I'm just an old woman struggling to get through the day. That's why I'm building this wall and this stone patio. I'm like one of my favorite poets who liked to work with stone."

"Was that Robert Frost? He wrote a poem about mending fences, putting the rocks back in place with his neighbor."

"Well, he didn't like building fences; it was his neighbor who said, 'Good fences make good neighbors.' No it's Robinson Jeffers. He actually went out and built stone walls like I'm doing. He's not well known; he's a little, well, a lot dark."

"Like you. Your poems are dark. Nobody but another poet knows what your poems are about. You're a poet's poet."

"Well, you know, Angie is a good poet. She gave me one of hers for Christmas and I couldn't figure it out at first. She had a lot of veiled allusions and then she explained some things. I was pretty impressed. She says she's writing quite a bit while she's at school."

"Are you going to stop building walls for the day and come in the house? I'm going to unpack and try to relax a little."

"Let me just get this one in place. Then I'll show you the drawings of the patio and wall I'm building. Can I ask a quick question? These slate steps are falling down and you know how much I like them. Can we get them repaired? I know we can't hire someone, but could you fix them? I really don't want to have to tear them out."

"It would cost a fortune to repair, and I could never do it. No, we have to rip them out and build wooden stairs. I'm sorry."

"Is that your final answer? The slate steps are so much a part of this old house. There's nothing we can do?"

He shook his head sadly. "I know what you mean, but I just don't see how it could be done."

# Chapter 16
# Cross Route 32

━━━━━━━━━━━━━━━━━━━━━━━━━━━━━━━━━━━━

It was a few weeks before Father's Day, the year after our Mohonk weekend. Rob and I were sitting at an outdoor table having seafood at Mariners Harbor on the Hudson River. "I have a gift for you. Let me run get it from the car."

Racing back, I tossed the box on the table.

"This is really neat, you don't usually give me a Father's Day gift."

"I know, but we've been dealing with so much stuff for so long, and we're not having much fun together. Go ahead and open it."

"It's in a shoe box, but I know it's not shoes. What is... Rhonda, what the hell, golf shoes? Golf shoes?"

"Look what else is in the box."

"Coasters to put my beer on?"

"No silly, look at them, they're not coasters."

"They say 'New Paltz Golf Club,' this one has my name and this one has your name...These are hang tags for our golf bags. Oh, my God, you joined the golf club?"

I was so excited. "Yep. You've been wanting to for years. We need something to do together. We have to have something besides talking about Angie. I can't stand it any longer. That's all we talk about. We need an escape. It's just not good for us to be so weighed down by this. Don't you agree?"

"Let's go now, today. We don't need tee times, do we?"

━━━

A little later that day, we were driving though New Paltz toward the golf club. And as always, we were talking about Angie. What were we going to do? Was she really going to go through with this surgery? Did she really know what she was doing? Did we believe she was really a girl? It was the same discussion we had every day, every year since she had told us about surgery.

As we crossed over Route 32 just a mile from the golf course, I had an idea. "Listen, this should be a time that we escape from talking about Angie. We can talk about her up until we get to Route 32, but once we cross, we have to stop. No discussion while we're playing golf. And while we're at it, no talk about work, the economy, paying bills, being sick or anything bad."

"That's a good idea. So starting now when we cross Route 32, we immediately change the subject. Deal!"

"It's a deal. And if you break the rule, you have to add a stroke to your score."

That was the only summer that we felt our budget would allow us to join the golf club, but we had a great time together. We became a close team as we walked the links, chasing balls and watching the sun sink down behind the mountains. We usually ended up at the bar for a quick beer while we joked with the other members. Occasionally we met other friends there. It was fun, relaxing; we were getting exercise, and we never discussed Angie or any other problem while we were there.

"Let's cross Route 32" became our signal to each other that we needed to change the subject or that we had beaten a dead horse concerning any subject. Both of us use the signal, and we both honor the request.

There have been times when we were screaming at each other in a heated argument. One of us said, "We need to cross Route 32." And we immediately stopped talking. We looked around, commented on the weather, the birds, the ten strokes it usually took me to get to the green, or we both just started laughing at ourselves. Crossing Route 32 has been our roadmap to sanity.

# Chapter 17
# He is not a girl

Rob and I began a marathon of movies and documentaries about transsexuals. Beginning with *The Crying Game* and its shocking revelation, we watched everything we could find. *Transamerica* is good; I watched the whole movie with my mouth dropped open, shocked, bewildered and weeping openly. We skipped the transvestites and cross-dresser movies; they are good and funny, but not at all related to being a transsexual. One documentary that was especially disturbing was about the many transsexuals who live on the fringe of society. Many had been rejected by their families. Many had botched surgeries and suffered terrible disfigurements. They purchased black market hormones and self-medicated. The more movies we watched and the more we learned, the more frightened we became.

We read everything written on the Web, in books, in medical literature. We were trying to understand. It just didn't make sense. *True Selves*, by Mildred Brown and Chloe Rounsley is an excellent book written for families of transsexuals. But I didn't read to find out how to help my child. I didn't read to learn how to support and help. I read everything I could find, to prove to myself that my child was definitely not a transsexual.

I kept reading the symptoms and telling myself that this was not my child. I was definitely the Queen of Denial. I told myself that if he had been a girl, I would have noticed when he was growing up. There was no way that something so important could have been missed. There would have been signs. He would have been effeminate, which he was not.

He would have dressed in his sisters' clothes, which he did not. He would have gotten into my makeup. The really interesting thing about how screwed up my thinking was, is that I'm not very feminine. I rarely wear dresses; I tend to dress rather gender-neutral. My life's uniform is turtleneck, bulky sweater, jeans and, oh how I hate to admit this—I still wear the Bass Weejuns I had in high school. How unfeminine is that? So why I thought he should have acted feminine is still a mystery to me.

But what I learned later was that Will had been wearing women's underwear for years. Angie told me that she had wanted to dress up, but there wasn't much to choose from at home after the girls left. Can't blame her there, my clothes are pretty dull and she certainly didn't want to dress like me. I think the honest truth is that I was looking for any excuse to prove to myself that he was mistaken, that he was not a girl. I was holding him to a higher standard than I held myself to. I was desperate to prove he was wrong.

And also to be honest, there were signs. I had forgotten about the Halloween he dressed as a girl and how excited he was. He had even told me he would prefer that the kids call him a girl. I just didn't think it could possibly be true. Truth sometimes just can't be grasped in its entirety; it has to be accepted in little bits and pieces over a long period of time.

One day I was working on my scrapbook, looking through pictures of our Taekwondo competitions. I found a picture of myself at the National competition, proudly showing off my gold medal. Will was standing beside me, hugging me. He must have been about ten years old.

"Rob, come quick. Oh, my God. You'll never believe this. Come here! Quick."

"What the hell is wrong? I hate when you scream like that. You sound like you've seen a ghost."

"Look at this picture. Look at the way Will is standing." He was leaning into me, with a crooked little grin. One knee was bent toward his other knee with his heel off the ground. "Just like a girl! Oh my God, how did we not see this before? Look at him!"

Rob grabbed the picture, stared for the longest time and slumped down onto the chair. He slowly shook his head from side to side. "Were we blind, or what? Oh, God, what else did we miss that was right in front of our faces?"

⟩⟨

I was helping Will put on his sparring gear. He was about twelve years old. It was a big competition, a local or state qualifier. "Are you excited?"

"Yeah, Master Klee said I would be sparring with a girl."

"What? That's not possible. The boys compete together and the girls compete together. Did you hear him right? What did he say exactly?"

Sighing heavily and rolling his eyes in disbelief, he enunciated each word as if he were talking to a four-year old. "He said, 'You are sparring with a girl. Her name is Angela and she is a black belt like you.' It's no big deal, Mom. You spar with men. I spar with girls. We do that all the time. What's the problem?"

"But this is a qualifier; she can't compete at Nationals in the boys' division."

"It just doesn't matter, Mom. Get over it. I'll be fine. I won't hurt her. She's probably better than me."

That was the strangest competition I had ever been to. I was the only person in the bleachers. "Where are the judges? What's going on?"

I watched in horror as the girl started off with a round-house kick to the head.

"Aggressive little bitch." They circled a few times and Will attempted a weak front kick. She easily blocked and knocked him on the floor with a side kick to the gut. He lay without moving. "Where are the judges? Get up, Will," I screamed.

She was standing over him, kicking him in the groin. But he just lay there with a sinister look, smiling up at her.

I tried to run to him but I couldn't move my legs. I began swimming in the air with my arms. "Will, Will," I screamed.

"Mom, Mom, wake up."

I blinked rapidly, shaking my head. I stared in disbelief. "Angela, you're the girl he was sparring with."

"Mom, what in the world are you talking about? It's me, Angie, you've never called me Angela. Are you having a bad dream? Wake up. Wake up, would you."

I blinked several times. "Yes, yes, Angie. It was just a bad dream, a very bad dream. I'm OK now. Come here let me give you a big hug, I love you so much. Now just go back to bed. I'm sure everything will be OK."

"Where's Dad?"

"He was called out on an emergency. He should be back soon. I'll be fine."

"Are you sure? You were really screaming."

"I'll get up and have a cup of tea. That always makes everything better. Go back to bed; I know you have to get up early for school."

I filled the teakettle, watched the flames leap to life and then leaned against the kitchen window. The old rippled window pane distorted the full moon. "You look like a skull, you old moon. Are you laughing at me too? I tried to raise a son, but somehow I failed."

Skull moon winks through pane,
Chest leaps, pulse quickens, palms weep,
Heart's work left undone.

# Chapter 18
# What's under the kilt?

"Look at you two. Rob's wearing a hat with a thistle and your ball cap has a rose. Aren't you a matching pair? I guess your ancestry is English, huh. How did you end up with this knucklehead, Scottish bozo? Turn around Rob; I've got to see that kilt."

Rob obediently began a little jig and bellowed: "Water is the strong stuff—it carries whales and ships. But water is the wrong stuff—don't let it get past your lips. It rusts your boots and wets your suits, puts aches in all your bones. Dilute the stuff with whiskey, aye, or leave it well alone." He grabbed a fried turkey leg from his friend and danced through the crowd roaring, "Ah, me buckos."

He had begged me to let him grow his beard for the Hunter Mountain Celtic festival we attend every August. "I hate your long white beard; it's really nice when it's trimmed close and you look like Con Hunley. You know you're just as handsome as he is. Promise me you'll trim it after the festival."

"I promise, I promise and I'll even buy you something at the festival. You want a tartan skirt? They make the cutest miniskirts for women, you'd look adorable."

"I'm nearly sixty years old. I will not wear a miniskirt."

"Why not? You have the body for it."

"Don't even go there. I'm not wearing a miniskirt."

"Well, we'll see. I'm buying you one anyway."

More of his friends joined us at the Hunter Mountain festival. "Come on, Rob, do your routine again. It's hilarious; really, you got to watch him. He had everyone around here laughing so hard they were crying. Come on, show us your stuff, you idgit."

"I'm going shopping." I shook my head and rolled my eyes. "Mary, let's go see the vendors."

"God, Rhonda, I haven't seen you two since the festival last year. How's Will?"

"How's Will? Oh, I don't know. He, uh, she. Oh, I don't know. I don't know, I just don't know."

"What's wrong? Why are you crying? Talk to me."

"He wants to be a girl," I blurted out. "He's having sex change surgery. Don't you know? I thought Rob had told everybody. It's been goin' on for years. I'm at my wit's end. I'm so confused. I'm angry. I just want to scream."

Mary's mouth dropped open, her eyes widened and she stared at me as if I were totally out of my mind. "What are you talking about?"

"I'm so sorry, Mary. I don't mean to just drop this on you. We've tried to tell everyone. But you know Rob, he has a million friends."

"I don't know what to say. How are you dealing with it?"

"Oh, God, not well at all. I've been a total mess for a few years. I just can't accept it. I feel if I accept it and it's a mistake, it will be my fault. I'm doing everything to prevent it."

"Rhonda, even if he's only twenty-two, Will is an adult. He has to make his own decision. It's not your decision. I've known him all his life; I know how he carefully thinks through everything. I'm sure this will all work out. You really can't make that decision for him. Come on, let's go shopping and you can tell me all about it."

"OK, you're right. It's not my decision. Why did I think it was? You're right. And you're not the first to tell me. Katy said exactly the same thing just a few weeks ago. I have to let go. Just...let go...Let's go find that miniskirt Rob wants me to wear!"

⚜

Every year we host a reunion of the PUDS, the Pelham Urban Development softball team from the 1960s. The PUDS and their wives come to our home for the weekend. Some stay at local motels; some sleep in our camper, in our guesthouse and in our house. We were gathered after dinner in the living room.

"Oh, my God!" I heard Katy screech. "You have a print of Joan of Arc. I have this same picture. You got it at the Met. Right? I've never known anyone else who has it. I love this picture. Come here guys, look at it. Have you ever seen it? You've got to go to the Met and see it yourselves, it's huge. Look at Joan. She's gazing into the sky, listening to the saints tell her what to do."

"And look at the saints in the background—looks like they show her masculine side and her feminine nature. She's like the perfect incarnation of all our potential. I bet Angie likes this, doesn't she?" said Kim, who had been studying the picture for a few minutes.

"How...how did you know?" I stammered. "You've never met her."

"Just from the way you describe her. Sounds to me like she's got that yin and yang figured out pretty well. She's going to be fine."

"You know what, Kim." I said, "I just met you today but I feel like we've been friends forever."

"What is that little brown wooden box with curtains?" asked Ruth Ann, my sister-in-law.

"That's what Rob gave me for my sixtieth birthday."

"You're not sixty, no way. I had no idea. You don't look it at all," said Kathy as she twirled her waist-length black hair."

"Well, this year I definitely feel it. I've never thought much about age, but this year it sure has hit me hard."

"So how's Angie doing? She looked great the few minutes that she was here."

"She's great. I've never seen her so happy. But let me show you the stage. Watch this."

I flipped a switch and the burgundy curtain opened. Tchaikovsky's *Nutcracker Suite* began to play. The miniature dancers twirled in time to the tinkling music. A minute later the curtain closed, opened again and another scene with different dancers moved across the stage.

"That's exquisite. I've never seen anything like it. Where did you get it?"

"I've wanted it for years. It's a Mr. Christmas Music Box. Rob asked if I wanted anything special for my sixtieth so I said this is what I wanted."

Just as the last notes tinkled, bagpipe music blasted through the room. The place exploded with laughter. Rob was prancing across the carpet in full Scottish garb. He danced and sang and joked for ten minutes.

"You'll see this on YouTube," Kim yelled out, "I've got my camera right here."

"Rob, stop it" I yelled. "You're being vulgar; nobody wants to see what's under your kilt. It's being filmed!"

But there's no stopping him when he begins a comedy routine. He was having the time of his life. He was surrounded by his best friends; they were egging him on and he certainly wasn't going to listen to me.

"Rhonda, go put your skirt on. Show it to 'em."

"Don't be ridiculous, they don't want to see my skirt."

"We do, we do," they cried in unison.

I shook my head and rolled my eyes. "OK, OK, you guys are crazy."

---

I pulled the purple and black Scottish National tartan skirt up to my waist and cinched it tightly. I carefully stepped into the black tights and pulled the black turtleneck over my head. I sat on the floor slipped my feet into the ghillies and slowly laced them. I was thinking of the day I had bought the little skirt. The day I knew I had to let go of Will.

"So, ma'am, for your skirt, do you want the McDonald clan tartan like your husband or do you want the Scottish National? We can make it either way."

"He really wants me to get the McDonald but I like the Scottish National. How is a skirt different from a kilt? They look the same to me."

"Same thing. A man wears a kilt, a woman wears a skirt. Unless she's in one of the drummers' or pipers' groups' then she wears a kilt. Fifty years ago there weren't many women in the groups, but now there are lots. So now I guess it's all the same. We're all cross-dressers," he said, laughing. "And nobody really cares what it's called. It's good to see the way people are these days. Nobody cares what's under your kilt. It just doesn't matter."

I placed my order for the skirt and walked slowly toward the crowd gathering to watch the hundreds of drummers and pipers march down Hunter Mountain for the grand finale. "It just doesn't matter...It just doesn't matter...We're all cross-dressers. All that matters is that a person lives a true life, feels comfortable with themselves and fulfills their destiny...It just doesn't matter." My eyes were drawn to the top of the mountain, just in time to see the grand marshal raise his baton to begin the jubilant march down the mountain.

And this time the drummers were not drumming a death march, like the day William told us he wanted the sex change. This was a lively, victorious, earsplitting bag pipe and drumming event with hundreds and hundreds marching in celebration down Hunter Mountain. Marching, laughing, occasionally stumbling and rolling from their drunken day of celebration—hundreds and hundreds filling the air with heartfelt joy—down the mountain toward a joyous life.

My chest no longer ached with the searing dagger of death. Will wasn't dead, I knew that now. He was the shadow cast by Angie's energy and bright life. He and Angie were one. They were together a strong, powerful energy leading a fight that would free a repressed and sad soul to fulfill a destiny.

And they also had shown me how to fulfill my destiny. I was following Angie's example in an attempt to become my true self. I was learning how to make friends. I was becoming more animated and opening my heart to the ones I loved. I was working toward my true life.

⇥⊹⇤

We had compromised on the length of the skirt—it was above my knees but not too short. I admired myself in the mirror. Not bad for sixty. And maybe I can start wearing more skirts and dresses.

"Debbie! That's the cutest little dress you're wearing. Wherever did you find it?"

# Chapter 19
# Expensive undertaking

"Ok, Ms. Rhonda, you're the mathematician, add it up."

"And you're such a smart ass. From my research, I have to say surgery could be anywhere from $50K to $100K. Electrolysis is $7K to $10K, hormone treatments $50 to $100 per month. Her Lamictal is $1,200 each month. How could she ever pay for it? What exactly did she say?"

"Her exact words were, 'Dad, I know you don't really believe that this is real. I know that you haven't accepted the fact that I'm having surgery, but I am having surgery, with or without your help.'"

"I had hoped she would change her mind. I thought she would see that it really isn't worth the trouble. But she has never, ever wavered. She did everything in the program, never looked back. She followed the Standards of Care beyond the recommendations. It's been four years. There's no way she's changing her mind. And now I'm beginning to understand and to accept her. I've tried to imagine the pain she's felt. We had a long talk the last time she was home."

"Mom" she said. "When I wake up every morning I cover my body so I don't have to look at it. I shave my entire body; that hair totally sickens me. I see this beard and wonder why it's here. I shower with my eyes closed. Then I have to get dressed, making sure all the bad parts are hidden. Every day, Mom. Every single day. I hate having this awful body. It's not me. And it doesn't matter if I'm called William or Angie. I still feel the same. I can't live like this. I know that I still have a long way to go, that I'm not totally a girl, but I'll get there. That's where I belong. God made a mistake. Now I have to correct it. It's really quite simple. Difficult, yes, very difficult, but it has to be done."

"That was the first time I felt the conflict and the pain. I began to see her as a separate person, a real person. She has so much insight into her own life. She really amazes me sometimes."

Robert took a long, deep breath and slowly exhaled. "We can't have a daughter with male genitals. Transsexuals have been murdered, raped, tortured. She's not turning back. She is going to live as a female whether she has surgery or not. How could she possibly do this without our help? What should we do?"

"She's proven to me that surgery is necessary. I don't fully understand it, may never understand, but I know we have to help her. I want to help her. I want her to have a life, not to be tormented by this terrible situation that she's trapped in."

Robert was nodding in agreement. Despite our personality differences, Robert and I have the same values, accept the same responsibilities and have never disagreed on child rearing.

"There's no other way. So how do we pay for it?"

"We have a few options. I could sell my stock, but the stock market is at its lowest in twenty years. I could borrow from my 401K, which is another bad idea. We have credit cards, definitely a bad idea. The best solution is a home equity loan. And also, I guess we won't be retiring next year."

"No. We can't retire," Rob said softly. "I have no idea how this will all work out. Somehow we'll get through and I pray we're doing the right thing."

"Oh God, me too. But why don't we cross Route 32 for the day."

We both sat in silence, nodding at each other with tears rolling down our cheeks.

# Chapter 20
# Through the valley of the shadow of death

As part of the transition program, Angie was required to notify her friends and family. She contacted many family members and all of her close friends, and she also contacted many of our close friends. Robert is gregarious and has more friends than most people. He is still in regular contact with friends he grew up with in Pelham, New York. He is very close with his brother and two sisters. He has worked for the New York State DEC for nearly thirty years and has friends he met the first year there. He also has friends from the eight years he spent in Oregon. It seemed an impossible task to make sure everyone was kept up to date with Angie's transition.

Everyone seemed to agree that telling the nieces, nephews, and children of friends who had known Will since birth would be the hardest. Each was told in turn, some by their parents, and some by Robert. The interesting thing was that young people these days are much more informed, tolerant and accepting than our generation was. The usual approach was to tell them that a family member they knew was going through transition and would have a sex change operation. In most cases, their response was, "Is it Will? Oh, OK. He always seemed like a lost soul."

We agonized for months about how to tell our grandchildren. Dr. Grant said that if it wasn't made into a big deal, the kids would be able to accept it. They came to visit us one summer when Angie was home. Jim was six and Billy was four. Angie's hair was quite long and she looked very feminine.

Rob said, "Jim and Billy, you remember Will?" They both nodded. "Well, Angie is Will's new name. Is Angie a girl's name or a boy's name?"

"Girl's name," they both said.

"So is Angie a girl?"

"Yep," they both screeched in unison. "So, Poppi, can we go ride our bikes now?"

Months later, Ally said they told her that Will was playing dress-up, but they thought that was OK, since they like to play dress-up. I guess we all have different levels of acceptance and understanding.

It was much easier for me to tell my friends. I have one close friend in the north, Carol Elizabeth, an oral surgeon who lives in Somerville, Massachusetts. I call her Carol Beth so she can have a Southern name. She and I have the same birthday and have celebrated together for twenty years. We got together for our fifty-ninth, I told her about the impending surgery, we cried together and then we started planning the biggest sixtieth birthday bash imaginable. We thought it would be great to have a big party just before I had to leave for Colorado for Angie's surgery. My closest friend from the south is Ruth Ann, my neighbor in the third grade, and I have been burning that poor girl's ears for years.

Telling my family was an altogether different story. I'm still considered the black sheep of the family—I don't live in the South, I didn't give Crystal and Allison family names, I was the only one who had ever divorced, and the only one to marry a damn Yankee. The thought of telling my three sisters and my parents would send me into a panic. I had delayed it as long as possible. But like my cousin Brian told me, "Life's like an old stubborn mule. You can't back it up."

First I visited my baby sister Sarah Evander, who looks like Vivien Leigh as Scarlett O'Hara, and in fact, she acts like

Scarlett—must be that feisty French heritage. Her husband, Stan, is a retired army colonel and was a Commander of Special Forces during the Viet Nam era. Rob was in the Coast Guard, so when Stan and Robert the manly men get together, they compete with war and hunting stories. Evan and Stan lived in Pennsylvania, so one weekend I went for a visit. They were totally shocked, but Stan said, "You know, some things just can't be understood, they just have to be accepted."

As difficult as it was to tell them, they were supportive. So with that much under my belt, I began to try to figure out how I would tell my parents and other sisters.

We decided to have a little vacation on our property in North Carolina. We planned a huge trip to NC—RV, pugs and all—just to talk to my family. We were staying on our property at Rourk's Landing on the Lockwood Folly River, the most scenic river in North Carolina.

I was sitting in the shade of the live oaks, trying not to hyperventilate, when my sister Jamey Lynn arrived. She is five years younger and we are the middle girls in the family. We fought a lot growing up and have never really reconciled. But she's an ordained minister, and that day, she was my strength and biggest supporter. I choked back tears as I blurted out the details. She sat very still for a long time and finally said, "I sure am glad I don't have to be the one to tell Mama."

After a long cry together, we slowly drove the few miles to my parents' home at Sunset Harbor on the Intracoastal Waterway. We were passing my sister Ruby's home just as she was walking over to my parents'. Ruby Ann is the oldest and recently retired from teaching. She's quiet, polite and mild-mannered. As we drove onto the white, sandy driveway and parked under the live oak tree, Mama came home from shopping.

"God, what timing," I sighed. "We're all arriving at exactly the same time and we didn't even have a set time to meet. Eerie."

"I can't believe y'all are here at the same time." Mama came running for a hug. She was excited to see us all together. "Whew! It's hot!"

"Yes, ma'am, it is," I said.

"When was the last time we were all together? I'll make some iced tea."

I found Daddy sitting on the pier, watching the boats go by. He's been retired twenty-five years but still wears an ironed dress shirt every day. He wears it with jeans and sneakers, but he cuts a dashing Southern gentlemanly pose since he's six feet tall, very slender with white hair.

"Can you come in the house? Mama just got home."

"Why sure, honey, anything for you."

We gathered in a little circle. Mama was still wearing her shopping "tenny" shoes, her mature-lady elastic waist pants and a hummingbird T-shirt that I'd bought for her at Cracker Barrel a few years earlier. She was rocking slowly and probably wondering what was going on. Ruby Ann sat demurely in her blue seersucker A-line skirt and flowered T-shirt. Her ankles were crossed above her Easy Spirit shoes and her hands were folded in her lap.

I stumbled through the details as best I could without totally breaking down. Since my parents are so religious, most conversations end unpleasantly with a remark similar to, "Well, now, if you and Robert would go to church and pray, I'm sure God would answer your prayers. You know you haven't brought up your children in the ways of the Lord."

I gave up a long time ago trying to explain that God is not in the church—that he's in the woods, the wind, the flowers, so I didn't even think about going there anymore. I waited for the response I had expected. Mama had stopped rocking. Ruby Ann sniffed softly into her monogrammed handkerchief. Jamey Lynn was squeezing my hand so tight I wanted to scream. But I just sat and waited...and waited, through the choking silence.

Finally, Mama said, "Y'all remember the last time Will was here? It was a few years ago. I don't know why you can't bring him more often." She stole a glance at me and I hung my head in shame. "Anyway, he was so quiet. He sat out on the pier by himself for hours, just staring at the water. I've never seen such a sad little feller. I knew then that something was wrong. Didn't I tell you, James? I must have been the first to notice. He seemed like a lost soul. Well, I'm so sorry, but it's nothing you and Robert did. He was just born that way. Angie, yes, Angie is a nice name. How is Angie doing?"

I was just about to faint when Daddy leaned over to me, hugged me and said, "I'll pray for Angie every day. Tell her we love her."

Ruby Ann said, "Tell her we will always love her, and we really want her to come for a visit."

Two weeks later Daddy called; he was all excited. "Turn the TV on. 20/20 is doing a special on young transsexuals. It's really a good program, I got to go, don't want to miss anything. Bye-bye."

I don't know what they really felt or if they have accepted Angie. They always ask about her when they call and they always invite her for a visit. I'm sure they felt some kind of confusion, some loss of Will. But in polite Southern society, problems sometimes just aren't addressed.

We Southerners are just not good at expressing our feelings. We'll skirt an issue, talk politely about any topic, but when it comes to true feelings, we just don't know how to get to the bottom of things. I want to take Angie for a visit. It has been so many years and we live so far away. I just don't have enough energy right now to introduce her to Southern society. But you know what—I think she'd make a damn good Steel Magnolia.

We'll have to plan that trip.

# Chapter 21
# To the brink of suicide: did I emotionally castrate my son?

And then one day, in the blink of an eye, the whole truth was out in the open—I finally knew what had caused my son to be a transsexual. The question I had asked a thousand times had been answered. And the answer was worse than anything I had ever imagined. He had known all along and finally, I knew the truth—I had emotionally castrated my son.

I was the worst female imaginable. I was the overbearing, smothering, horrible, controlling mother who had destroyed her only son. I had done the unthinkable. I wanted to die. There was nothing left for me.

The hot bath scalded my legs and it didn't matter. I hoped the running water would drown my sobs and occasional gasps as I pulled hanks of hair out of my head and bit my tongue to keep from screaming. I grasped my knees, hugging them to me. I rocked and rocked and rocked. I could hear Robert down in Angie's room, saying, "Talk to me, I'm here to help you."

Angie's sobbing became louder and louder. "Let's talk. Please Angie, let's talk. Please tell me everything. Just keep talking. We'll work it out. Please tell me everything. Tell me everything. I know Mom loves you. Tell me everything." Robert repeats himself when he's nervous. Over and over he kept begging Angie to talk to him.

I couldn't hear what they said next, but it didn't matter. Nothing mattered anymore. My life was over. My own words kept bashing inside my head: "I did it. It's all my fault. I caused my son to be a transsexual. I castrated my own son and now he's a transsexual."

He was small for his age. His uncontrollable seizures began when he was a few months old. He had a learning disability, and didn't learn to read until he was eight. He had been sexually assaulted at age six; he had emotional problems. But I never knew until that day that he hated me and blamed me. I had no idea that I had hurt him. And I knew for sure, most of what Angie had said was just not true. I never, never did all of those things. He didn't wet his pants. If he did, I never knew about it. He had occasionally wet the bed. I never, ever called him stupid. He had been very sensitive as a child, and any discipline would result in hours of crying. But why was she making this stuff up? Why would she say those things? What did I do to cause this?

It had all started so innocently. Angie had arrived home for Christmas break from SUNY Cobleskill where she was a sophomore. It was our first time together since Robert and I had accepted the fact that our twenty-one-year-old child was going to have sex change surgery. She was excited to begin the electrolysis that would remove her beard; we had lots of appointments set up for the Christmas break. We had meetings with her regular therapist, Dr. Thomas Grant, who had diagnosed her with Gender Identity Disorder. We were going to see Donna Festa, the gender therapist at Westchester Medical Center, who had been treating her for several years; and hopefully we would see the endocrinologist to start hormone therapy.

Angie was thrilled that finally, after all these years, she had convinced us that she was truly a girl and needed genital reassignment surgery. We were moving forward. She was more talkative lately. Robert said that she chatted continuously all the way home. Now it was late evening and we were all exhausted from this long-anticipated visit home.

She was standing at the foot of our bed. We were all three actually having a conversation, our first in many years. Just casual talk, laughing together about how difficult the years had been and how we all knew we had hurt each other's feelings. She had written an article for the school newspaper called "Openly Transsexual at SUNY Cobleskill." I had read it, focusing on the part about how her parents had rejected her. That part was mostly lies, stuff she probably had read about other transsexuals who were rejected by their parents. We had not immediately accepted that she was a transsexual—it took about four years to begin to accept it, but we had not rejected her. Robert had confronted her about the article and told her we were pretty pissed about the things she'd said. I could see how she might consider our slow process of acceptance a rejection, but I dismissed the lies as poetic license. I didn't think much about it. We continued to talk about feelings and dealing with all of the problems.

I'm not a very talkative person, but I added my bit to the conversation by saying, "Yeah, my feelings were hurt last summer when I thought I was having a heart attack and asked you to call an ambulance and you said, 'Why don't you call it yourself.' I was really surprised," I continued, naively expecting her to apologize and say how she didn't mean to hurt my feeling. "I felt you didn't love me."

The deadly silence was frightening. She tensed and straightened to her full five foot six inch height. Her upper lip quivered. I watched in amazement as her green eyes narrowed and I heard the poltergeist utterance.

"I didn't care." Her lip rose in a sneer "You could have died and I wouldn't have cared." Her face contorted, she clenched her fists and her body shook as she continued. "You ruined my life. You treated me like shit my whole life. You told me I was small. You criticized me when I wet my pants; you told me I was stupid. And you want to know what the worst was?"

She leaned toward me and shook her fist. I pressed my back into the headboard, my heart pounding. I held my breath. I stared into a face I had never seen, a red, menacing caricature of someone I didn't know. Her chest heaved as she stammered. She grasped her head and swayed back and forth. A pathetic wail rose from deep inside her. "I've hated you my entire life," she hissed. "You! You!" She choked and sobbed, "The worst you did was...you...you yelled at me when I told you I had been molested. You yelled at me!" Her voice had grown louder. "You told me it was my fault. We were driving to school and you yelled at me and said it was my fault. Steve didn't hurt me, he was my friend. He liked me. I liked him. He was my friend! But you! You hurt me."

"Oh my God," I thought, "she's calling her molester her friend. He was a child predator." "But, Angie," I tried to inter-ject. "That's not how it happened. In the car, when I yelled at you, it was for something else. You told me about Steve in the kitchen at home."

"I remember it like it was yesterday." She was now indig-nant. "You yelled at me and said I caused it to happen. We were in the car and you were yelling. You!" She clenched her teeth and pointed at me, her eyes narrowing as she leaned in. "You caused all the pain that I've lived with all my life. My life is fucked up 'cause of you. Nobody has ever hurt me like you did. I hate you." Calmly and deliberately, she now emphasized each word. "When that ambulance came, I watched from the window. I saw the stretcher leave. I was smiling when they drove off. I hoped you would never come back."

My bath water was now ice-cold, their voices droned on and on. I couldn't find any reason to continue living. For the first time in my life, I seriously contemplated suicide. How could I have caused my child all of this pain? How could I have been so blind and cruel? And how could I have ever thought that I was a good mother. "What have I done? Where did I go wrong?"

"Come on out." Robert was pulling me gently out of the tub.

"No, I just want to die. I caused all of this. She hates me. I'm the reason Will wants to be a girl."

"Don't be ridiculous. You didn't cause this. She's very upset, but we talked a long time."

"Why did she say all those things? Did I call her stupid, ever? I would never call her stupid. Tell me, did I do all those things she said? I just want to die. This is all my fault."

"Stop it. Stop it, now!" Robert was shaking me. "Now listen to me. She told me that she can't remember lots of things and gets them mixed up sometimes because of the seizures. She said she doesn't know why she blames you or said all those things. I suspect she may have read about them happening to someone else, and because she can't remember her own life, she thinks it might have been her that they happened to. You never called her stupid. I don't remember her wetting her pants in school. I know for sure she is mad at you for yelling at her about something related to Steve and the sexual abuse."

"It must be my fault that she's a transsexual."

"Now listen and listen good." Robert glared at me. "She believes that she was a girl from birth. She doesn't think that anything caused her to be a transsexual. If you keep saying that you caused this, then you will undermine her belief that she has always been a girl. She needs to be able to believe in herself."

"What can I do?" I sobbed.

"Go down and talk to her. She loves you and needs you. You know that every girl hates her mother and blames her for everything. You have two other daughters; you should know that by now. What did Oscar Wilde say?"

I smiled weakly at Robert. "That children love their parents, then judge them, and if they're lucky, they forgive them."

Robert led me by the hand down to Angie, who was curled up with her baby blanket and favorite stuffed animal, Brave Heart Lion. We all cried for a long time. We didn't talk, but I vowed that I would do everything in my power to try to make her pain go away. The pain I had caused, the pain the world had caused and the pain Angie had caused herself.

And she was right about one thing. Years ago, I yelled a lot about one problem. I was a broken record back then. "William, where did you get that Game Boy? You cannot keep borrowing these games from your friends. I've told you so many times. What if something happens—a game gets broken or lost and we have to pay for it? Take this game back to your friend and don't borrow any more."

Months later, shaking and sobbing, he had told me about his friend who gave him the Game Boy. In great detail, he told me what the older friend had done to him, hiding behind his backpack in the rear of the school bus. I'm not a psychologist, but I can easily see why years later he remembered that I yelled at him about the Game Boy and associated it with getting molested.

There was no reason to even suspect that I would sleep that night after our confrontation. For hours and hours I lay in bed, replaying the horrible night in my mind. How could I have been so cruel and thoughtless? Was I really as bad as she said? Every parent says things that hurt their children. Was I worse than most? And what about Crystal and Ally? Did I hurt them, too?

Finally, I gave up on sleep and in the darkness pulled on my turtleneck, bulky sweater, yoga pants and thick wool socks. I slowly plodded down the spiral staircase, and at that moment I heard the light switch on in Angie's room. I gasped, fearing that she wanted to scream at me some more. I stood motionless, listening to my heart pounding.

Tentatively, I knocked on her door. "Do you want to join me for tea?" I expected a gruff "No!"

"Sure," she said in a small whisper.

I let the teakettle fill to the very top, knowing that the more water I put in, the longer it would take to boil and the more time I had. I didn't want a confrontation. I wanted to try to somehow apologize. I kept formulating and then rejecting my speech.

I dropped the strainer into the teapot and added two pinches of my favorite white tea. I scrounged through the cabinets for the Scottish shortbread I kept hidden for special occasions.

She was curled up deep into the overstuffed leather sofa with Brave Heart Lion and her well-worn baby blanket, which was held together with safety pins. She rubbed the satin trim slowly between her thumb and forefinger.

"Here's your favorite Care Bear mug. Do you want sugar or honey?"

"No, thanks."

"I-I guess you didn't sleep much last night either," I stammered. She just shrugged. "I want to tell you how sorry I am for ever causing you pain. I know it doesn't matter whether I meant to hurt you or if it was an accident. It must have hurt you a lot." She nodded in agreement, so I continued. "Parents can be really stupid sometimes. They think they are helping their kids by reprimanding or correcting them. They even try to protect their children from hurting themselves. I know I've made lots of mistakes. You just didn't come with an owner's manual."

I watched her smirk slowly widen into a grin. "I had a lot of problems, didn't I? I guess I'm pretty unique."

Feeling bolder, I went further. "I know you blame me for things, and I definitely understand. It's OK to blame me.

I really didn't know what I was doing a lot of the time. Especially in the last few years as you began your transition."

She shook her head slowly. "No, Mom. I don't blame you. I blame myself, but I took it out on you. You're an easy target. You take everything so seriously. You did say some things that hurt me. The problem is that when Dad says things, he is just off the cuff. He says the first thing that comes to mind. Then he back-pedals for fifteen minutes, apologizing and trying to explain what he meant. But when you say anything, I know you've thought about it forever. You don't say anything unless you know you're right. And that's the problem. Sometimes the truth hurts."

"You're an adult now and have been for a few years. I've been wrong to try to tell you how to live your life. From now on, I'll treat you as a friend instead of my child. I've learned that I can trust you to make your own decisions. Is that OK with you?"

"Yeah, that's OK. You know, Mom, I really don't regret my life. As difficult as it's been, it's what made me what I am today. And I really like myself now. If I hadn't had all these horrible problems, I wouldn't know anything about myself. But I feel I really know myself. Lots of kids at school come to me for advice. Isn't that just incredible? I was the Ugly Duckling, but now I'm becoming a swan and they all recognize it. Maybe I'll be a teacher or a psychologist."

"You'd be good at either one. You have really amazed me. I know it has taken me a long, long time to accept you and the surgery, but I want to let you know that I really have a lot of admiration for your courage and fortitude. I know you have been through hell. I can only imagine how horrible it has been for you to feel that you're in the wrong body. I'm so sorry you've had to endure this. And I'm especially sorry that I was not strong enough to help you through this."

We watched the sun come up together that morning. She told me horror stories of her last few years and the transition. She said probably one of the most difficult parts was always finding a family rest room out in public. She explained some of the strategies she had to employ to make sure she could get through an outing in an unfamiliar public place. We finished off another pot of tea and all the cookies. She seemed more at ease. I felt that it was the first time she had truly shared her life with me. I was blessed to have had the chance to listen to her.

# Chapter 22
# Who else did I hurt?

A few days later, I was beginning to feel I was getting back on solid ground when Angie's older sister, Crystal, called. I braced for an onslaught of criticism. "Hi dear, how's Madison?"

"We're both fine, Mom. But what's this I hear about Angie having surgery? Have you and Dad agreed to pay for that? This has gone way too far. You are being manipulated by her. You are paying for her hormones and her surgery. She's so young. How does she know that she won't regret this?"

"I've thought the same thing. When I was her age, I didn't know what I was doing. But think about yourself. How old were you when you ran away to work on a horse farm? How old were you when you flew down to North Carolina, established residency and then got a full scholarship to UNC? You did that all by yourself. She's trying to be herself, just like you. You two are so much alike. Do you know that you even look alike? She won't let us take many pictures, but we had to send one to Dr. Bowers, and I'm just amazed how much it looks like you. And you're both opinionated little, how does Angie say it? Bee-otches. You know you weren't easy to love either, when you were young."

Crystal laughed, "Yeah, we're all bee-otches, aren't we?"

"I agree."

How many times had we heard that we babied Will, that we had done too much for him his entire life? And now, how dare we help Angie with this totally unnecessary surgery? Children in their thirties will still compete for Mom and

Dad's attention. And they will swear we never did anything for them.

Unfortunately, there's a lot of truth to Crystal's allegations. We didn't do as much for them. We had no money when they were growing up, and she was totally right: I was consumed with caring for Will. As she stated so succinctly, "You didn't seem to care one way or another how I was going to fare when I was his age. I'm not saying you shouldn't take care of him. I'm just sad that I didn't get the same care and concern."

I closed my eyes and dropped my head back letting her rant as long as she needed to. Angie wasn't close to her two older sisters. Crystal was twelve and Ally was nine when Will was born. They adored their baby brother. But now they both lived out of state and had spent little time with Angie. In fact, Crystal had never even met Angie.

"But Crystal, we're just doing what we think is best. Do you know how dangerous life is for a girl with male genitals? Transsexuals have been murdered. We just can't have a daughter living with a male body. I don't understand any of this either. I wish it wasn't happening. And I'm sorry you feel that way. I'm sorry we didn't do more for you. I really want to try to make it up to you. Why don't we talk some more later?"

Slumping onto the sofa, I eagerly accepted the comfort of my two little pugs who nestled close to me. "I love you. You're so easy to love. No strings. No tuition. No running off to join the circus."

Not only did I feel that I must have in some way caused all of this angst, I felt that I was being blamed for not stopping it. I must somehow be responsible for my children and all of their problems for their entire lives. I thought kids were difficult when they were young, but life with adult children seemed to be getting much worse.

I stiffened as the phone rang again. Caller ID showed it was Ally. Exhaling loudly, I clicked the phone to speaker. "Hi, Ally, how are Billy and Jim?"

"We're all good. What's happening with Angie? Crystal said she's having surgery. Can't you do something to stop her? Are you really paying for her hormones and for surgery?"

Would this nightmare ever end? "Listen, Ally, I know you're upset. Are you sad because you're losing a brother, or is it something else?"

"I just don't understand why this is happening. Angie is all you think about and talk about anymore. We haven't seen you and Dad for quite a while. What about your grandchildren? Do you ever think about them? They used to have an uncle, but he's gone and they don't know who Angie is."

"Stop crying, please. Can we talk more the next time you're here? Let's all just hope she changes her mind. We still have time; she can change her mind and be a boy again."

Of course I knew that wasn't possible. I knew she wasn't going to change her mind—not Angela. She was a headstrong, opinionated, young woman. She was so unlike poor little William, who was a sad, frightened, downtrodden child. "But, remember, she is William," I chided myself. "She is the strength that he developed. She is the same person, just different wrappings. William is now a strong, assertive individual who knows what she wants in life. My child has balanced that yin and yang. My dear child has turned travesty into triumph."

---

My morning routine rarely varies. I'm up before the sun and the birds. While Petey and Laiha, my sweet little pugs, greedily gobble their breakfast, I do my morning stretches and prepare my pot of tea. Every morning I have a full pot of Darjeeling Silver Tip white tea, which comes from India. It is hand harvested from buds and young leaves. It's the only luxury I allow myself. I buy it at Tealuxe in Harvard Square when I visit Carol Beth who lives near Cambridge. We stroll from her house to the square, peruse the bookstore, have lunch at the Thai restaurant and then, buy my six-month supply of tea. She also sends me a refresher supply for Christmas.

It was Sunday morning, the first weekend of spring 2010. Two feet of snow had been dumped on us two weeks earlier, causing the largest power outage in the history of our area and plunging 150,000 of us into darkness for six days. By now, it had nearly melted. I was totally alone. Angie was visiting friends for the weekend. Rob was in Oregon, visiting friends he hadn't seen for fifteen years.

The pot of tea was ready. Petey and Laiha were following my every move, jockeying for their positions on the sofa. As soon as I sat down and covered myself with the blanket, they were on my lap. Petey had never sat in my lap until after Laiha came to live with us, and even now when he wanted to sit with me, it was only to be close to Laiha. So finally they settled down, one on each side of me.

This was my quiet time. Each morning I eagerly anticipate the sun's rays sneaking through the trees on the mountain. The gossamer pink blankets the valley, slowly fading into mauves and then gold. This is my time to sit for an hour or two, to watch the sunrise, watch the birds scrounging at the birdfeeder, listen to the Woodstock wind chimes and hear the waterfall just outside my living room window.

I saw a cartoon many years ago of a girl sitting which read, "Sometimes I sits and thinks and sometimes I just sits." As hard as I tried, I could never "just sits." I think too much. I've always wanted to turn off the constant chatter, the stream of "what if this happens" or "what am I going to do about that." I've tried meditation, yoga. But nothing allows me to "just sits."

It was unusual that I was home that weekend. It was the traditional weekend for my trip to Carol Beth's house. It was the weekend for our sixty-first birthday celebration. She and I have gotten together each year for the last twenty-one years to celebrate our birthdays. But her travel arrangements had gotten screwed up somehow, and instead of going to Tibet and then back home to Cambridge, she was in Bhutan, a tiny independent country in the Himalayas which borders Tibet. According to Business Week, it's the happiest country in Asia and the eighth happiest in the world. It's reported that the country's leaders feel that Gross National Happiness is more important than Gross National Product.

So on that morning I was thinking about happiness, or more appropriately, the lack of happiness. Many years ago I heard a saying that a mother is only as happy as her unhappiest child. I couldn't remember a time when I actually had happy children.

Crystal, who is now thirty-six, was totally destroyed by my divorce from her father. It had been a horrible, bitter divorce which ended by him telling her that if she wanted to live with me, then she would never see him again. Unfortunately, he meant it. I had realized within a year of marrying him that he was incapable of giving love, that he thought he was a god because he was a physician. I never understood the cause of his arrogant disdain toward all humans and his cruel treatment of his own family. Ally had little memory of him, and pretty much told him to go f___ himself when she asked Rob to adopt her. But Crystal had held onto the hope that he would someday be her dad again.

She tried to keep in touch with him for years. She wrote, called, sent him information about her life, and invited him to her wedding. She got nothing but rejection in return. She took her anger out on me. She also hated me for not spending more time with her. She resented having a younger sister, and then when Will was born and required my total commitment, she rebelled. At fifteen, she ran away from home. Fortunately she didn't go far. She took a job on a horse farm and lived there, helping with the chores.

She finally returned home to graduate from high school, only to climb into a two-seat, single prop and fly to North Carolina, where she has lived ever since. As she got older, we began to repair our relationship; it was difficult since she refused to discuss anything with me. She just wanted the problems to be over and to love each other now.

She came to our home in Highland a few years ago. Angie was off at college and Rob was working, so we decided to go to NYC for the day. We live ten minutes from the train station, so we hopped on Metro-North at Poughkeepsie and settled in for the hour and a half ride to Grand Central.

"You know, this is the first outing that you and I have ever had—just the two of us."

I tried to grasp what she was saying. "What do you mean? Our first outing together?"

"You and I have never, ever had a day together—just the two of us. It's really sad."

I was trying to figure out how that was possible. She's the oldest, so from the time Ally was born, if we did anything, it would have been with all of the children or the entire family. "You're—you're right." I stammered. I could feel the embarrassed flush rising up from my toes and creeping over my body like a shroud. "I never thought of trying to make time just to be with you. I'm sure that has been painful for you. I'm so sorry."

"But we're together today, Mom. It makes me happy, and you're going to show me Joan, right?"

"Yes, we're going to see Joan of Arc. So, you've never seen the painting?"

"No, never, which surprises me since I have a degree in art, and I've been to the Met many times. How did you learn about it?"

"It hangs in the hallway by the Impressionists exhibits. I walked out of the main exhibit one day into the hallway and was totally overcome by it. It's huge, nine feet by nine feet. And the look on Joan's face is ethereal."

"And it's your favorite painting? And you're taking me to the Met just to show it to me?"

"Yes, yes. A whole trip to NYC just to see a painting."

Leaving Grand Central, we headed toward Fifth Avenue and began walking toward the Metropolitan Museum of Art. It took about forty-five minutes but we enjoyed the stroll. About halfway there, we were walking through Central Park when it suddenly became very dark, and we heard thunder. We looked up just as the sky opened and a brief shower interrupted the otherwise sunny day. We started laughing and running, arriving at the museum totally soaked. We were dripping from our heads, down; our clothes were soaked through to our underwear. And we couldn't stop laughing.

I paid our admission; we snapped on our little buttons and headed toward the ladies' room, still giggling like two drunken schoolgirls. We stripped down and began drying our hair and clothes under the hand dryers.

"What happened?" The concerned patrons surrounded us.

"We got caught in the downpour."

"It was totally sunny when we came in."

"And it's sunny again."

Finally, somewhat dry, we headed upstairs to see Joan of Arc. Crystal gazed at her without moving. Then she walked closer, then farther away. Finally she moved into the doorway of the Impressionists, all the while shaking her head and murmuring. "Yes, yes, it's marvelous. How did I miss this in all my trips to this museum and in all my art history classes? I just love it. This will now be one of my favorites."

"Did you want to wander around the museum a bit?"

"No, I'm so overwhelmed by this that I don't want to look at anything else. We came to see your favorite painting, and now it's my favorite too. I'm so glad we came."

Crystal and I were happy that day together. We were also happy the day Maddie was born. I was holding her hand, watching as the doctor held up my beautiful granddaughter and carefully placed her in Crystal's arms. "I'm so glad you're here, Mom."

Two days out of a lifetime together. How did I fail my child so terribly?

The teapot was empty. Petey and Laiha were snoring loudly. I wondered if I would ever be able to make it up to her.

She struggled to understand and accept Angie. Then she found a way to express her anger and frustration. She called me one day to say that she had been keeping a journal for many years and had decided to go public with a blog. Before she went public, she wanted me to read it, especially the part called "The Christmas of the Box."

The Christmas when Angie and I had our terrible confrontation was so hectic with the many doctor and electrolysis appointments that I had put Christmas on hold.

"What are you sending the girls for Christmas?" Rob always left all of that to me, so I was a little surprised that he was even asking.

"I just can't handle it this year. I've been trying to think of something to send; I haven't even gotten the grandkids anything. And I just remembered that I didn't even send their birthday gifts. I think they're still in the closet. This just isn't like me. I'm totally losing all sense of control. Can't you send them something? Ally and her family are going to North Carolina to visit Crystal for the holidays. Why don't you send something for everyone to Crystal's house? None of them needs anything, just send a little something to let them know we're thinking about them. We'll try to make it up to them next year. They know that we have a million things to do to get ready for Angie's surgery."

So, after agonizing for several days over what to send, Rob, who loves food and all things related to food, decided to send a boxed set of gourmet Christmas desserts. It looked lovely, all stacked up with each box individually wrapped. At least in the catalogue picture, it looked really nice. "Everybody loves food. Don't you think they'll love this? The grandchildren can eat the cookies; the adults will love the fancy cakes. I would love to get something like this."

He was very excited and called them every day for a week. "Did you get it yet?" Finally they got it, but were less enthusiastic than he had expected. "Oh well, I tried."

"You did fine. If it had been up to me, nobody would have gotten anything." I didn't really think much more about it until I started reading Crystal's blog a year and a half later.

"Oh my God, Rob, come here."

"What's so funny? Show me. Is it Crystal's blog? It better not be bad. This stuff is going public, you know."

Rob didn't want to read her blog. It was just too personal, and her anger at me was too apparent. But I pored over every word, trying to make sense out of our lives together. I wanted to find out where I had gone wrong and find ways to correct it. By now I was laughing so hard that I was crying.

"You're crying. Is it bad? Just tell me, I don't want to read it."

"You have to read it, I can't explain it."

And unfortunately I can't possibly explain it as well as she had written it. The story was called "The Christmas of the Box," and the gist of the story was that for Christmas that year, our daughters had learned that their baby brother was going to have genital reassignment surgery. And apparently, when they opened their gift box of desserts, one of our sons-in-law said, "So, let me see if I have this right. Your brother is getting a very expensive vagina, which, if

I can be crass, is called a box, and all eight of us got this cheap little box."

Her blog went on to say that by the next Christmas, we had more than made it up to all of them. And that she was very happy with her family.

I had gone all-out the next Christmas. I love Christmas and love to give gifts. So I spent months and months picking up special gifts for everyone. We all gathered for a great celebration and all thoroughly enjoyed being a family. I had made my first big step in trying to reconcile with my children.

# Chapter 23
# That looks ridiculous

Angie refused to take fashion advice from me, or from anyone else for that matter. She loved her fishnet that she had worn since her trip to Washington, DC many years earlier. She now had a complete wardrobe of black and red fishnet—tops, glove thingies and stockings. I hated it. She swore that she would wear it for the rest of her life. She wore it every single day.

She was also very big into the Goth look with the black lipstick and black nail polish. She wore very heavy eyeliner and dark eye shadow. Trips to the mall for school clothes were exasperating. I would pick out nice blouses, sweaters and pants, and she would smirk and shake her head.

I just wanted to smack her sometimes, and shake some sense into her. It was bad enough she wanted to have her own style, but these clothes were ridiculous. She was adamant that she definitely wanted her own style and would not listen to me. I bought fashion magazines to show her and pointed out girls we passed that I felt were nicely dressed. She stared at me in disbelief, lifted one eyebrow and just laughed.

"Mom, please. I know what I'm doing. Just leave it alone. I know how to dress."

Our usual shopping haunt, even from the time Will was a young child, was the Poughkeepsie Galleria. I spent many, many hours sitting alone on the marble stools while he played arcade games.

"How's your ice cream, Will?"

"Great, I love these little frozen ice cream dot thingies."

"Who was that girl you were playing video games with?"

"Just a girl from school."

"Do you like her?"

She's OK. Well, yeah, I like her a lot, but she hates me."

"Hates you? What do you mean? She seemed friendly enough. She's really pretty with that long dark brown hair. And you know her eyes look a lot like Crystal's."

"You think she looks like my sister?"

"Yeah, something about her reminds me of the way Crystal looked at that age. Are you thinking of asking her out? What's her name?"

"I told you she hates me. Her name's Angela. She told me once she wanted me dead."

"Oh, no way. She was probably just kidding. Listen, I just have to run into the ladies room. I'll be right back."

The thought of a girl saying she wanted to kill him was distressing. I quickly dried my hands and raced back out. "Will! Will! Where are you?"

"Will!" I screamed.

"What's wrong, lady?"

"My little boy's missing. I think he's been kidnapped. He's very small, eight years old. Some older girl named Angela said she wanted to kill him. Help me! Help me! Somebody help me!"

"Oh God, Mom. Not another nightmare. What's wrong with you? Why do you keep having nightmares? Wake up and tell me what's wrong."

She was shaking me gently. "What's wrong, Mom?"

"Oh Angie, I just keep having nightmares. I've had them since you told me about having surgery. I thought I would get over them. But they just won't go away. I guess I'm still sad about losing Will. At one time I had a little boy that I loved very much."

"And you still have that little boy, Mom. He's still here with me. I've learned to love him and to accept how much he did for me. He was so brave. He was teased and tormented for so many years. But he was strong. He kept me safe and he brought me into the world. I don't hate him. I love him and I've decided to honor him. Do you want to know what my legal name is going to be?"

I smiled weakly and nodded.

"I've thought about this for a long time, and I'm going to name myself Angela Williams. I picked Williams to honor the little boy, William, who kept me safe and protected me all those years. I didn't want to tell you before 'cause I wasn't sure, but now I'm very sure and that will be my legal name. Can I have a hug, Mom?"

"I love you, Angie."

"And I love you too, Mom."

# Chapter 24
# Fashion advice

Probably the most painful, difficult, time-consuming and expensive part of the transition from male to female is removal of the beard. The only way to permanently remove the beard is laser or electrolysis. Laser is considered a permanent reduction, which means eventually most of it grows back. Electrolysis is considered permanent, but only after each hair follicle has been zapped three to four times over a period of many months. It can take at least 100 hours for a beard to be removed, and the surgical area also has to be cleared. We estimated that it would cost $7,000 to $10,000 for hair removal.

Angie doesn't drive since she is terrified of having a seizure. I knew I would be driving her for all of her appointments. I had never known of any electrolysis salons in our area, so I was dreading having to take her into Manhattan for treatments which would add considerably to the expense.

Dr. Bowers, who was Angie's surgeon, has a website with links to professionals trained in electrolysis for the transsexual. I was fortunate to find Linda Weller in Newburg, New York was recommended by Dr. Bowers. It was only a half-hour drive, much to my relief.

Angie was very nervous. "I know it's going to be painful; how will I tolerate it? I'm going to spend a lot of time with this woman. I sure hope she's nice."

"She sounded very professional and concerned when I called her. This will be a consultation, and then she said if you're ready, she'll just start with fifteen minutes."

"Oh, I'm ready all right. I want to get rid of this beard; it's so hard to hide with makeup."

We drove the half-hour down Route 9W onto Route 32 in Newburgh. "This is it. Look at that little red house, isn't this just the cutest little office you've ever seen? I guess we'll be seeing a lot of this place over the next two years."

It was summer vacation, so we scheduled appointments two to three times a week for the entire summer. She began with fifteen minutes and then eventually worked up to ninety minutes. I would drop her off, drive to a shopping area, wander around the mall, read in the car, sit in the parking lot of a restaurant, talk to family members on the cell phone, pay bills, make lists—or sometimes I would just sit and cry.

She would come out a session, slump over in the car seat and moan with pain. Her face would be red and swollen for a day. And then we did it all over again, and again and again. We didn't talk too much. Neither of us is talkative, and during those years we had reached an unspoken agreement that we were better off not talking, since it almost always ended in some kind of screaming match.

She usually came out of the session with a fashion magazine that Linda had given to her. She said that Linda advised her on dressing and makeup. I hoped she would heed Linda's fashion advice since she certainly didn't listen to mine.

One night I was watching *What Not to Wear*. "Angie, can you come here a minute? I want to show you something. Have you ever seen this show?"

"No, you know I don't watch TV. What kind of ridiculous outfit is that girl wearing?"

"Well, that's the point of the show. She thinks she looks great, so her friends contact Clinton and Stacy. They secretly tape her, surprise her and then they show her how she can get the look that she's trying for. Why don't you watch with me? I really like this show." So we watched as the girl wearing pink fluffy boots, skintight pants and an army jacket was transformed into an attractive yet still interesting person, with her own quirky style.

"How do they do that?" She sat staring at the TV.

"The most important thing is that they want to understand what she is trying to say about herself. Not just in the clothes she wears, but how does she feel about interacting with the world. What does she want to accomplish? Then they apply a few rules, and they are very clever at finding pieces that work together to achieve an overall look. Most of the girls balk, complain, swear they will never change, and then at the end of the show they are absolutely thrilled with the changes. Don't you think she looks really feminine? She has a quiet, yet strong confidence. She seems to stand taller and looks happy. She knows she is dressing her body in the best styles, flattering but not flaunting. She acts like she could do anything she sets her mind to. I think that's true femininity."

"I want to be unique, different from everyone," Angie said.

"You are unique. I don't think unique means weird, different or isolated. What makes each of us unique is what we don't know—our own ignorance. Nobody in the whole world doesn't know all of the things that you don't know. It's what you don't know that makes you unique. And to develop your uniqueness is to get rid of your ignorance. That's why education and new experiences are so important. You are chipping away at your ignorance. I guess my theory is like a photographic negative of what most people consider unique. You don't have to work to be unique; you have to work to develop your uniqueness which then brings you closer to other people."

Her eyebrows shot up and she smirked. "Mom, has anyone ever told you that your thinking is a little weird? I'll really have to think about that, but you know what? I'd like to have a makeover. I'd love for Clinton and Stacy to tell me how to dress."

"Me, too," I said. "I've never been able to dress very well. I'd love to go from dowdy to dashing. Would you like for me to contact the show and recommend you?"

"Well, yeah. That would be awesome. And I'll recommend you. Maybe we could go together."

So for two years now I've kept an eye out for Stacy and Clinton, hoping they will grab me and offer to throw away my wardrobe. I keep waiting and watching, hoping I'm being secretly taped. Angie on the other hand, has made amazing strides since her surgery. She has followed Linda's advice and is developing a confident feminine style. She wears many different colors. She mixes vests and sweaters with frilly blouses. She wears formfitting slacks with her knee-high leather boots. Her skirts are not too short. And I haven't seen any fishnet since her surgery.

Linda became a great friend and resource for Angie. One day Linda asked her if she would like to meet another woman who was having treatment. She was a patient of Dr. Bowers' and was working as an advocate for transsexuals. Angie met with her and asked a lot of questions about the surgery, and how the woman had felt about having the surgery, and about Dr. Bowers. Angie said that meeting her was really beneficial and answered a lot of her questions.

One day we were driving home; I was lost in thought and she was silent as usual. Her soft voice broke the silence. "It sure must have been difficult for you to raise me. I had epilepsy, had trouble in school, I got picked on and bullied. I must have been a lot of problems for you. And now look at all the things you still have to do for me. I don't know how you do it."

The road ahead was a total blur. I slammed on the brakes to avoid running off the road or running into another car since I was blinded by the sudden rush of tears. All I could manage to mutter was, "Well, we do what we can." And the silence returned.

# Chapter 25
# Hormone hell

In the United States the Standards of Care have strict guidelines for transsexuals who desire surgery. They must live full-time in the new gender for a minimum of three months and provide a letter from a therapist before beginning hormones. Angie had been living as a female for several years before she began the hormones.

Angie was referred by Donna Festa, the gender specialist, to a clinic in New York City, Callen-Lords. Angie and Rob took the train to NYC, where she met with an endocrinologist for the first hormone prescription. The options were pills, the patch, or injections. Angie chose injections.

The hormones were sent to her school nurse, who administered the injection each month beginning in early 2008. Angie was so excited, but unfortunately the excitement was short-lived. She called us regularly to keep us updated. "It's horrible. For three or four days I can hardly function. My life is out of control. I can't concentrate in school."

She told us that she could barely get her schoolwork done. We had no idea what to do. We still hoped she would change her mind and not have the surgery, and we also knew that within a few months, the hormones would cause her to be sterile. She had chosen the injections rather than pills because the pills would go through the liver; and with all the seizure medications which had gone through her liver, she thought an alternative would be better.

After a few months, the injections had become intolerable, so she opted for the pills. She has taken them now for nearly three years with no adverse reactions. She will continue them for the rest of her life.

We knew when we agreed to the surgery that the insurance would not cover the surgery or the hormones. One day when I went to the pharmacy for the estrogen, the pharmacist suggested we submit a claim. "Insurance companies are changing. Why don't we just give it a try?"

We waited anxiously a few minutes. "They approved it," He was grinning from ear to ear. "You just never know until you try."

With that victory, Robert and I decided to see if the insurance would cover the surgery. Robert's medical insurance with New York State is considered the best employee medical benefit available. We submitted a predetermination, and the surgeon, Dr. Marci Bowers of Trinidad, Colorado, submitted all supporting documentation showing that Angie had followed the Standards of Care and that she had the necessary letters required for the surgery.

In the United States, the patient must be eighteen, and in most cases must have had hormone therapy for one full year. Two therapists must send letters to the surgeon attesting to the need for surgery.

We had paid Dr. Bowers in full for the surgery, but we kept hoping the insurance would pay some portion. I was in constant contact with a supervisor at the insurance company, but we had not heard anything for more than a month. I waited anxiously every day for word.

Finally, we got the official word that the insurance company had approved the surgery and would pay a portion. We were ecstatic. It didn't matter how much they paid—when you have a $50,000 surgeon and hospital bill, anything helps. There are some people who feel that gender reassignment surgery is elective surgery and should not be paid by insurance. I wish it were elective—a choice. But unfortunately, it's not elective surgery, if there is a choice for transsexuals; it is to choose to live a true life with body modifications—or to choose suicide. This is a recognized medical condition similar to a birth defect.

When we met with Dr. Bowers, she told us how surprised she was that the insurance would pay. She said that most insurance from other countries throughout the world will cover the surgery, but in the United States it is extremely rare that her patients have coverage.

Hopefully, more employers will understand that this surgery is not optional or cosmetic, but is medically necessary, and they will begin to allow coverage for their employees and family members. Most people who have group medical coverage through their employers do not realize that it is the employer who decides what is eligible for benefits, not the insurance company. I spoke with other patients while we were in Colorado and encouraged them to go to their human resources department, to get the support of the health benefit administrator who can encourage the company to cover medically necessary surgery.

# Chapter 26
# Pug heaven

I have two of the cutest, loudest-snoring, most adorable pugs in the whole world. Princess Laiha and Black
Creek Pete give me joy every day. They brighten the worst
hours. They squeal with delight when I enter a room. Laiha
sounds like a little wind-up doll and Petey tries to bark but it
just comes out like a cough. They run around in circles, vy-
ing for my attention. In her excitement, Laiha spins her little
circle out of control like a helicopter just before it crashes
to the ground. She then falls over and Petey pounces on
her, licking her eyes and ears till she nips at him. They greet
me with the sweetest, most caring kisses when I walk in the
house, whether I've been gone for two days or two minutes.
I can't sit without Laiha climbing into my lap and immediately falling asleep. Without them, I surely would have high
blood pressure and all of the illnesses that I imagine I have,
be the meanest person on earth and hate to wake up every morning.

Petey was our gift to Will when he earned his black belt
in Taekwondo. He and Rob researched breeds for about a
year before he decided that a pug was the dog for him.
"They're kinda funny-looking, don't you think, Mom? Did
you see the way that tiny one came over to me? I liked him
a lot. He has the most character. Did you see the way he
tilted his head and listened to me when I talked?"

We waited until we moved from our off-the-grid home
in Red Hook. Will was not ready to move from the only
home he had ever known. He loved the farm; he loved being outdoors and driving the tractor. But he hated his school
and the bullying he had been a victim of for years. He was

much stronger now that he had studied martial arts and self-defense, but kids are cruel, and some of them never changed even if they suspected that a black belt might just beat the crap out of them.

It was not long after we moved that we bought Black Creek Pete, named for the Black Creek that runs through our property. Will was ecstatic. He held him like a baby and wept for joy.

"You know, Mom I noticed that if I sit with him while he's eating that he seems happier. But if I walk away, he stops eating. It's like taking care of a baby. Don't they tell you that you should always hold them to feed them and not leave them with a bottle propped up?"

"Didn't you tell me that you wanted to enter the science fair this year and needed an experiment? Why don't you do an experiment to see if he really does eat more when you sit with him?"

For the next few weeks Will ran several different types of experiments. He carefully measured the feed before and after feeding. He would sit with Petey and talk to him softly for some feedings. Other times, he would just put the feed down and walk away. And sometimes he would sit for awhile and then, get up and walk away.

He kept meticulous records and then began to construct graphs and charts to show the results. He took pictures of Petey and along with the graphs and charts made up his science panel board. He got clearance from the school to bring Petey in his crate to the science fair.

"I know it won't win or anything, but I had a good time doing the project. Do you think that since it's not mixing chemicals or something, it's not really a science project? They might not like it."

"This is science. It's behavioral science, called psychology. Psychologists have to conduct this kind of experiment with animals and people all the time."

"Really, you mean I was doing a real science project?"

His project was a huge success. The judges said they had never had that kind of experiment, and that it showed creativity. It took the grand prize for the fifth grade. It was a great way to begin his new life at his new school.

"Maybe I'll be a psychologist when I grow up. Wow, this is really neat."

It wasn't the first time that Will had showed great insight and in-depth thinking. A few years earlier, Rob and I had separated for about eight months. The off-the-grid lifestyle had been extremely difficult and had put a strain on our marriage. We had talked for years about selling and moving somewhere closer to civilization. I am a loner and love privacy, but living and maintaining the house and also caring for Will and his many problems had proven more than I was willing to accept any longer.

One night we were going over the same old ridiculous arguments. Neither of us would budge. There was no hope for reconciliation. We wanted opposite lives and there could be no compromise. Will, who was about twelve at the time, walked into the room, stomped his foot, slapped his hands on his hips, and rolled his eyes. "You two are just ridiculous. I wish you could hear yourselves. You're both saying the same thing, just different ways. You're both wrong. Can't you see that?" He tuned abruptly and stomped out of the room.

We both burst out laughing. The next week we began marriage counseling, thanks to our Little Buddha, as we started calling him.

So to help him with his transition to the new school, we had gotten Petey. He and Petey were close buddies for a few years. But when Will began puberty and his dark years, he neglected Petey. They were no longer the best of friends. Will was irritable and moody and Petey was just a bother.

I loved Petey and had always wanted a lap dog for myself, but Petey didn't care anything about sitting with me. He just pined for his lost buddy. He moaned softly, sighed heavily and jumped up expectedly when he heard some-one, but then just flopped back down, dejected.

I decided that I wanted to adopt another pug. I want-ed a lap dog and Petey needed a companion. I didn't want a puppy, since small dogs are more difficult to house-train and pugs are notoriously stubborn. It had taken a year for Petey to be house-trained. I spent hours on the adoption Web sites, looking for the right pug. I applied and anxiously waited to be approved. I had to tell them all about our dog, our home, yard, income. I knew we were the ideal home. A few weeks later, I received word that our application had been rejected because we had a dog that was not neu-tered.

"Well, no, he's not neutered. He's a show dog, a pure-bred stud." I knew that all of the dogs they put up for adop-tion had to be neutered, so why would they care if my own dog was not neutered? "He's a house dog, for Christ sake. He can't get out and get any dog pregnant, and why would I neuter a pure bred, champion-line show dog? If your dog is spayed, he certainly can't get her pregnant."

My objections fell on deaf ears. They had their rules and according to them, any owner who didn't neuter their dog was irresponsible and would never adopt one of theirs. I was disappointed, but let it go. Petey and I sort of existed together. Not buddies, but we just hung out together.

A couple of years later I heard Rob talking to someone from his office on his phone. "She did a few years ago, I don't know about now. But it might be good for her. You know how upset she is with Will, I mean Angie, going through this transition."

I was trying not to eavesdrop, but I was leaning closer and closer to the closed door. Suddenly it flew open. "Do you want a pug? The owner died last month, and his kids have seven children and can't take care of the dog."

I planned to pick her up on my way home from work. I was so nervous to meet her. What if she didn't like me? She was seven years old; she could have all kinds of medical problems and might not be house-trained. And she might not get along with Petey. They agreed to let me take her on a one-week trial basis. It would give Petey a chance to get to know her. I had an appointment with the vet. Nobody even knew if she had been spayed.

I sat on the floor, waiting for the seven children to release her to me. She waddled over, struggled to get into my lap and then sat snorting and staring at me, with the absolute ugliest puppy mill face I have ever seen. Her owner had fed her cookies, so she was at least eight pounds overweight. She was snaggletooth and bug-eyed. She started snorting and coughing and I thought she was going to die in my arms. Her blotchy black and fawn coat felt like a bristle brush compared to Petey's smooth fawn coat. Her tiny petal ears were lopsided; her tail was screwed too tight. It was definitely love at first sight.

I called Rob on the way home. "I love her. I love her. Take Petey outside so they can meet on neutral territory. I should be home in about ten minutes.

"What the hell? Rhonda, that is the ugliest dog I've ever seen. And she's so fat she can hardly move. What have you done?"

"Let's see how they get along. Keep Petey on his leash; I'll let her go on her leash a little at a time. I think they like each other. Let's take them for a little walk up the trail before we take them in the house."

Petey was prancing and sniffing. He licked her ears, her eyes; he wouldn't let her out of his sight. It was love at first sight for him too. And it has continued that way for nearly three years. He cries if I take her for a walk without him. He runs from one window to another so that she is never out of his sight. She likes him too, or rather tolerates his attentions, but she is my baby. If I even approach the sofa, she is on it, ready to sit on my lap and go to sleep. She wants to sleep with me and tries to hide so I won't put her in her crate at bedtime. She has lost all her cookie fat and looks very healthy. My two pugs have been my salvation.

About two months before Angie's surgery, they began to do the most annoying things. Petey would tangle himself around a tree every time we went on a walk. Laiha would jump up on me every time I got close to her. They barked at everything, they begged for treats, they became so annoying that I couldn't tolerate being around them. I would yell at them constantly. I yanked their leashes, pulled them in all directions. "What is wrong with you two?"

Then one day it occurred to me that they hadn't changed at all; they were doing the same things they have always done. They did the silly, crazy dog things that make them endearing. They were not being annoying. I was just totally irritable. My anxiety level was increasing every day.

I began taking long walks and hot baths, I prayed every day for strength and understanding, and I listened to soothing music. I joined a kickboxing aerobics class. I sang. I danced. I played my violin. Nothing helped. As the surgery day approached, I became more and more anxious. I was having heart palpitations, chest pains, and difficulty eating and sleeping.

I had planned to work at my job until the Friday before the day we were to leave on Tuesday, May 18, 2009. I thought it would be good for me to have something to keep me busy and take my mind off the surgery.

Well, I thought wrong. My last week of work was impossible. I had done everything I needed to do to get ready to leave for Colorado; I had nothing I needed to do at home, so I was available to work, but I just couldn't do it.

My job was demanding. I was a customer service representative for a health insurance company. I took calls from customers who either needed information or had a problem with a claim. I handled about eighty calls a day. I could tell how the calls would go by the first words out of their mouths.

"You people did it again!" was almost always a really bad sign.

"Get your supervisor on the line this minute." was OK, 'cause then I could just transfer to a supervisor.

"I don't know if you can help me" usually meant it was going to be a long, complicated problem, and no matter how many times I explained what a deductible was, they remained clueless.

"My wife died a month ago" sent me into a deep sadness, and I needed to have a good cry after the call. The other calls required that I give out precise, detailed information which could be very complicated and must always be accurate.

By the last week I was trying to work, my anxiety was so bad that I became afraid to answer the phone. I felt I was so distracted and anxious that I wasn't sure I could give the correct information. I began to second-guess everything I said. I would call my supervisor or one of the specialists to clarify facts that I had known for years. I couldn't remember the definitions of the simplest terms. I would get off the phone and wonder if I had told the caller the amount for the deductible, or if I had said it was coinsurance. I would transfer a call and then wonder if I had transferred to the right department, disconnected the call, or just left them sitting on hold.

Robert has always told me that he can tell where I have been—that anything I do, I do the best that can be done, or I don't touch it. I have to be the best; I don't accept anything less from myself. So not being able to be at my best for my job was really upsetting me.

I became terrified that I would give out incorrect information. But what scared me more than giving out the wrong information, was how I might respond to an irate caller. I was afraid I might tell someone what they could do with themselves and their claims. I began to imagine myself saying, "F___ you, asshole. Get a life and don't call me again. Didn't your mother teach you any manners? Have some respect for those of us who are superior to you. You are an L-O-S-E-R. Get off my phone."

How many times could I hear "You people," or "You are a total incompetent," or "I'm calling the Better Business Bureau, the Attorney General's office and the Department of Insurance," without totally losing my cool and telling them what I thought? It took a lot of finesse to get through a call with an angry customer, to explain how claims were processed, to get them to the department that could correct the problem while they were on the line. I wasn't sure my Southern charm would sustain me through this kind of call.

Each morning I would stare at the phone before I could log in to start taking calls. I would take deep breaths, pray for patience and guidance and then begin the day. By Wednesday I was still functioning but getting pretty shaky. And then I got the call to end all calls.

"Good afternoon, this is Rhonda. May I have your name, please?"

"How do you spell that? Is it Rhonda with an H, or was your mother ignorant and spelled it R-O-N-D-A? And what is your last name?"

"My last initial is A, sir."

"I don't want your last initial. What is your last name?"

"Sir, I'm only required to give my last initial, which is A. How may I help you?"

"Well, Ms. Smarty, Rhonda A. You people really did it this time. We better get this resolved today or you will hear from my attorney."

"May I have the date of service? What day did you see the doctor?"

"I was in the hospital on March 8."

"The date of service for your doctor's claim is March 8, 2009, is that correct, sir?"

"Isn't that what I said? Are you incompetent, or what?"

"I just need to verify the information, sir. What is the doctor's name?"

"It's for the hospital, you moron. I told you I was in the hospital."

"We process your claims for the doctors, sir. You will want to contact Blue Cross for the hospital claim."

"I have the paper right here that you sent me, showing you didn't pay the right amount to the hospital. What do you mean you don't process my hospital claims? I called the phone number on this paper and I got you. Now find that claim, damn it."

"Sir, you called the correct phone number, but after you call the number, you will want to press option two for Blue Cross for your hospital claims."

"Your phone system sucks. I don't have time to listen to those ridiculous options. Who is the incompetent moron that set up the phone system?"

"Your employer set up the phone system, sir. We have nothing to do with the phone prompts."

"My employer? What the hell are you talking about? This is my insurance company; I pay a lot of money for this. You are my insurance company. What does that have to do with my damn employer?"

"Please do not curse; I'm trying to help you."

"You couldn't help me if you tried, which you certainly are not doing. I asked you what does the phone have to do with my employer."

"This phone line is for your medical benefits, which are set up by your employer. Your employer determines all of your benefits and chooses which company processes your claims. We don't make that determination."

"Unbelievable. You're just trying to get out of taking responsibility for paying my claims. Why didn't you pay this hospital claim?"

"We only pay the claims for the doctors. Blue Cross pays your hospital claims."

"Then why didn't Blue Cross pay this one?"

"I can't speak for another company, sir. You will want to speak with Blue Cross."

"What do you mean, you can't speak for another company? You are my insurance company. I pay a lot of money for this insurance, and now you're telling me you don't pay my claims? I want to speak with your supervisor right now. And don't give me any lame excuse for not transferring me. I pay good money for this insurance. You're all a bunch of losers, incompetents, and uneducated morons. I'd like to have a job like yours where I just sit on my ass all day and read stuff off charts. Why would anybody ever hire such incompetents?"

"Please hold while I transfer your call to a supervisor."

I sat there for the longest time second-guessing myself. Did I transfer to a supervisor? Did I disconnect the call? In the last few weeks I had transferred more than one call to the wrong department. I was anxious; I was not functioning up to my standards. Could I have disconnected by mistake instead of transferring? Did I do the right thing, or did I do what I wanted to do...? Oops.

I called my supervisor. "Andrea, you've been so understanding these last few months, but I just can't function any more. I have to take the rest of the week off."

"Don't even worry about it. Go. Go. You've got a lot on your mind. You know, I just got that call you transferred to the supervisor line–what a nut! I wish I could take the rest of the week off. Do what you have to do. Keep in touch while you're in Colorado and let us know how the surgery goes. Come back as soon as you can."

"Thanks, I'll be back in a couple of months. If you don't mind, tell Jens and Ginny I'm gone and thanks to all three of you for your support. I'll keep in touch."

I took the rest of the week off. Petey, Laiha and I went for long walks. We got tangled around trees, walked through mud, barked at frogs, chased birds. Laiha tried to roll on a dead turtle, Petey wanted to eat something really gross; Laiha tripped me and I hurt my ankle, Petey scared some poor chipmunk nearly to death; Laiha found skunk scent and rubbed it on her back, Petey got tangled around a tree—again. We sang and laughed and just had a damn good time. They were themselves again.

Three months after we returned home from Angie's surgery, I heard her talking in the living room. I didn't remember hearing anyone coming in the house. She kept talking and talking. I was trying not to eavesdrop, but I was very curious.

"Yes, you are so sweet. I've missed you so much. But I'm back now, we're still buddies."

It was then I realized that she was talking to Petey.

"Come here. Let's play with your toys. And yes, you too, Laiha, you can play too. Wow, your coat feels really soft. You were like a bristle brush when Mom got you, but now you're soft like Petey. Must be that good dog food Mom feeds you. Oh, you two are just the sweetest things in the whole world. You knew I was coming back, didn't you? I've missed you, but now we can be buddies again. Well, that is, if you can get out of Laiha's sight. Or we can all play together. I'm happy now. Can't you tell? I was unhappy for a long time, but now I'm happy. Now I'm me. I love you and I love me."

# Chapter 27
# Exotic butterfly

I watch a little TV in the evenings. *The Closer* with Kyra Sedgwick as that Steel Magnolia is my favorite show, and yes, I'll admit it, I like *American Idol*. Rarely do I watch TV during the day. But one day I was watching *Oprah*. The show was about transsexuals, so it's possible that I had heard about it and intentionally watched the program. Oprah introduced a surgeon, Dr. Marci Bowers, who practices in Trinidad, Colorado. Dr. Bowers was a transsexual; had genital reassignment surgery ten years ago and now specializes in the procedure. That's how I found Angie's surgeon.

After doing extensive research, I contacted Angie and had her check out Dr. Bowers' website. "If you like what you see, I'll send the application with the deposit. Hopefully she'll accept you as a patient."

Angie was accepted and surgery scheduled for a year and a half later. We started the countdown. I began to do what I do best, which is planning. There was so much to do, from getting the therapists to send their letters, to deciding where we would stay in Trinidad. I had to find a kennel to take the dogs for two weeks and find someone to watch our house; we needed plane reservations, rental car and hotel reservations. I began making lists and then lists of lists.

There was also a countdown on Dr. Bowers' website that Angie had to follow. Angie had to have electrolysis to clear the surgery site. She had to have medical clearance from her neurologist; she had to meet with Dr. Grant and the gender therapist, the endocrinologist and she had to stay in school.

She studied the website regularly to make sure she was doing everything she was supposed to do. "Mom, do you think that my vagina will look real?"

"I'm sure it will look fine. Didn't you see the pictures on Dr. Bowers' website? She shows lots of examples of her work. They look pretty real to me."

"Yeah, I saw them, but, well, uh, well, since I've never seen a real one, I don't have any idea what one looks like."

I literally fell down, I was laughing so hard. "I'm sorry, Angie; I'm not laughing at you. It just never occurred to me that you didn't know what a vagina looks like. I honestly had never thought about whether you had seen one or not. Come here, girl, you deserve a hug. Listen, the truth is that most women have probably never even looked at theirs, and have no desire to look at it. Don't worry; I'm sure everything will be fine."

When we first started planning our trip to Colorado, just Angie and I were going, but after much discussion and by the kindness of a family benefactor, we were all able to go. We considered taking the train, which is a three-day trip, or maybe drive our RV or fly. We decided to fly. I hate to fly and had not been on a plane in thirty years, but it was the best choice. We made our plane reservations with plans to arrive two days before the surgery.

One morning during my usual "sit and think about everything" session, a month before the surgery, I realized that our reservations had to be changed. We had to make two connecting flights with little time in between. What if even one of them was delayed? Already we were scheduled to arrive close to midnight, and then drive two hours from Colorado Springs to Trinidad. Angie had to meet with Dr. Bowers at 9:00 a.m. the following morning.

In a panic, I called Robert. "We have to change the plane reservations. We can't take the chance of missing our flights and getting to Trinidad late. This is Angie's biggest day; we can't risk anything this important."

Robert contacted the airlines immediately and changed the flights to one day earlier, to the tune of a $700 increase. But it was worth it.

⊲|⊳

On Monday evening we were cleaning out Angie's dorm room. She had taken all of her exams early since school didn't end for another week. "Mom, Dad, I want you to meet Ricky, my very good friend. She's going to help us pack up my things."

I was sure Angie had said "she," but this was obviously a boy with long hair. As we drove away, I asked, "Is Ricky a transsexual?"

"She's just beginning. I met her a few months ago, and you know that I'm pretty well known on campus. She wanted my help. She's having a lot of trouble with her parents. They are totally against it, threatening to kick her out of the house. They're not accepting like you and Dad have been."

I stole a glance at Rob, who looked as shocked as I felt. Had she forgotten the years and years of arguing and pleading? Or maybe there hadn't been as much as I imagined. Maybe all that fighting was going on inside me—I had waged war with my own fears, doubts and insecurities. She, on the other hand, had been the picture of confidence. She had no battles to fight, just a lot of very difficult work. She had nothing to prove. She knew what she was doing. Was everything OK now that we had finally accepted her? Had she forgiven us for doubting her at the beginning? It seemed that way to me. Maybe we had cleared the air when we agreed to help her with the surgery. I breathed a deep sigh of relief. "And maybe I'm not such a bad mother after all."

"Yeah," she continued. "I told her that she couldn't force this major change on people, she has to give them time. I told her that other people have seen her as a boy all her life. They couldn't be expected to just all of a sudden start saying she's a girl."

Rob's eyes were about to bug out of his head. I didn't know whether I would laugh or cry or sing Halleluiah. But it sure was a great way to begin our trip to Colorado.

On Tuesday, May 19, 2009, at Stewart International, a small, easy-to-navigate airport, we boarded our first of three flights. Security clearance was quick and we were on our way.

"Ladies and gentlemen, this is your captain."

I nearly went into shock. My first flight in thirty years, I was terrified to fly and our captain couldn't be more than twelve years old. Where was Sully when I needed him?

Somehow we got to Detroit and I found myself in the future. The floors were moving, the airport was a shopping mall, and everyone was pulling little bags, running through the airport and talking on cell phones. And I'm sure I remember that thirty years ago, all of the Delta gates were in the same terminal, or at least close to each other. We were running from Gate A1 all the way to the other end of the airport; it must have been to Z26. We barely made our connection.

I was panting, standing in line and clutching my carefully packed, previously measured carry-on bag, when I saw the McFrequent Flyer Family. Dad had two huge bags on each arm. Mom had the biggest diaper bag ever constructed and was pulling a cart that had three bags stacked on it. Each kid had a huge rolling cart and the contents of an entire toy chest in a separate bag.

I watched to see if they would be turned away, reprimanded, get their bags measured, or what exactly would happen. But there was no comment from any airline employee. It was then that I realized the carry on requirements were just suggestions. I was the fool who had actually fol-lowed the very strict suggestions. And then I saw the va-let check-your-bag-at-the-door of the airplane, and then grab it as you leave the plane. "What the hell?" I thought. "I could have carried so much more shit!" But I guess I prob-ably had enough.

And then we continued to Minneapolis. And that air-port was exactly the same. Two major changes from thirty years ago: 1) No Smoking, which is really great, and 2) No screaming kids, not so great. There are screaming kids, but these little jets are so noisy that you simply can't hear them, or anything else.

Finally, about midnight, we arrived at Colorado Springs. We checked into the Comfort Inn, where I promptly threw up due to a migraine. What a long, horrible day we had en-dured. But at least we now had a full day to recover before Angie had to meet with Dr. Bowers. It was definitely worth it to leave a day early.

Next morning, we drove two hours from Colorado Springs to Trinidad, a tiny Western-era town in southern Col-orado on the Santa Fe Trail. We had struggled with where we should stay in Trinidad. Dr. Bowers' website listed hotels, motels, bed and breakfasts. The thought of spending two weeks in a hotel or motel was appalling. On the website, there was a listing for a private home on Robinson Ave that was available to rent. We decided that we would be much more comfortable there. Rob could cook, we would have more room to spread out and we'd feel more at home. In January 2009, six months before the surgery, I called the owners and reserved the house for two weeks.

We rented a car with Enterprise, and much to Rob's delight, they upgraded us to a Subaru Outback. "This is so nice. I was imagining us crammed into a little economy car. Finally we're here; I've programmed the GPS to take us to the Robinson Avenue address. Oh, shit, there's construction at our exit and a detour. That always screws up the GPS."

"Trinidad's pretty small, so we should be able to get there anyway," I said.

So our entrance to Trinidad was round-about. We finally started going in the direction of Robinson Avenue. "This isn't possible; we're already going out of town again." His tone told me he was getting cranky.

"So, Rob, just calm down, we'll find it. But first we have to cross Route 32. OK? Calm down and cross Route 32. The bitchin' isn't helping. We have to be really close. I'll just read the directions again instead of using the GPS."

"Mom, what are you talking about, cross Route 32? You and Dad say that all the time. What are you talking about?"

"It's just our signal to each other to change the subject or stop complaining."

"You guys are weird, but whatever."

"Oh, yeah, up this little road that we have passed three times. Here it is. Isn't this the cutest little adobe house you ever saw? It's better than the picture. And look at the view of the mountains. I like this already. I'm so glad we didn't get a hotel. Nice. Rob, here's the lockbox combo; I'll run next door to see if Nick and Tammy are here. They said they would be here today."

We met the owners, moved in and then spent hours talking to them about Trinidad, sightseeing, Dr. Bowers and the surgery. Their little adobe cottage is available full-time for use by Dr. Bowers' patients and their families. They have furnished it with everything needed. They also made up books with directions to the hospital, Dr. Bowers' office, shopping, and restaurants. They had tourist pamphlets for all areas of interest and directions for day trips.

While we were there, they were completing the work on the house next door, which would also be available in the future for Dr. Bowers' patients and families. We didn't see them again since they were returning to their home in northern Colorado, but they kept in touch during our stay and have kept in touch since then.

We were so thankful we had chosen to stay there. All of the other patients asked where we were staying and they all said that they were envious, since they had wanted to rent the house and it was already rented to us when they called.

We moved right in and felt very much at home. It was a small, quiet neighborhood just a few miles from the hospital, near a restaurant that served breakfast. We spent every evening sitting on the front porch, watching the ever-changing colors on the mesa. It also didn't hurt that there was a well-worn path to the liquor store down the hill. We definitely needed to go there.

Trinidad is called the sex change capital of the world due to the reputations of Dr. Bowers and her predecessor. Mount San Rafael hospital is tiny—only seventy beds. We were on a first-name basis with the entire hospital by the end of the two weeks, including the ER staff who let us in at midnight to deliver treats to Angie. The hospital is also well-known for a huge ceramic wall mural hand made by a nun. It is a history of the area and is worth a trip to Trinidad in and of itself.

Despite her fame and expertise, Dr. Bowers displayed genuine concern and provided thorough care for Angie and for us. "This is a family event; everyone gets involved," she said as she waved us into the examining room. She saw us every day, answered all questions and addressed all concerns. She kept Angie laughing as she cracked jokes on every visit. "They really had a note on your college dorm registration—NO ROOMMATE ALLOWED? Well, there you have the title of your book. You are writing a book aren't you, Angie?"

The office manager, Robin assisted us for months before the surgery. Janet was very helpful with the predetermination and the insurance billing. They have kept in close contact with Angie, answering questions for months before the surgery and for months afterward. They called several times following the surgery to make sure she was recovering and to see if she had any concerns.

Dr. Bowers and her partner also have a beautifully restored home for patients to use after their surgery. They even provide transportation for patients from the airport and around town. I felt genuine concern and caring from all staff members we met. I highly recommend Dr. Bowers to anyone contemplating this surgery.

After I saw Dr. Bowers on *Oprah*, we did extensive research and discovered that she is the best. She has patients from all over the world and is booked far ahead. And she is quite the media sensation.

When we arrived for Angie's first meeting the day before the surgery, there were already several reporters and cameras on scene including a crew from MTV. We had been notified that they would be there and were given the option to meet with them. We could decline pictures or filming, and no one would bother us. We declined, and they were very respectful. Robin had asked if Angie would like to meet with T Cooper, a writer who was doing a story on Dr. Bowers.

Driving from the airport, I had given Angie a printout from the Internet about T Cooper. He, previously she, is a novelist and writer for the New York Times and other publications. Angie chose to meet with him.

The following day, after she completed her preadmission work at the hospital, we dropped her off at the Tarabino Inn to meet with T Cooper. They talked for about an hour while we explored the Western-era town where Wyatt Earp was once the marshal.

I had stopped worrying about whether she would feel this was a mistake. She had convinced me that there was no going back, no regrets. All of my research had confirmed that almost none of the transsexuals who had surgery ever regretted the decision. The only regrets were those of ones who could never afford the surgery or who lived on the fringes of society. There are problems for patients with botched surgeries from incompetent surgeons who left them scarred for life. That's why we had chosen Dr. Bowers. She is the best.

I looked up to see her standing in the doorway, her long blonde hair draped casually over her T-shirt. She was wearing shorts and sneakers. She's a slim, stunning fifty-year-old; no one would ever know she was a male until ten years ago. Her quick smile is contagious and she has a great sense of humor. "It's a girl. And she did very well. You can go down to her room, and she'll be coming out of recovery soon. I'll see you every day."

When we walked into Angie's room we were greeted by her roommate, Anna, and her roommate's friends. "Great, so glad to see you; I get the young pretty one as my roommate. This is my wife, Zoe, and my personal photojournalist, Jan. When we saw your daughter in the waiting room yesterday, I said I hoped she would be my roommate."

While we waited for Angie to be brought to the room, we chatted easily about her surgery, which had been early that morning, and about her transition, which had begun after many years of marriage and five grown children. We were welcomed as members to an elite group, a group we had fought for years not to join. Her story was like that of so many transsexuals who wanted for years to transition, but tried to avoid it, only to face the possibility of suicide before finally transitioning.

When Angie was wheeled into the room, I was overcome with relief. "Hi, baby girl. You're here. You're finally here."

She grinned sheepishly. "I'm a girl," she whispered. "I'm the long-awaited princess."

"Yes, yes, you're our exotic butterfly. You look good—sleepy, but good."

"I'm shleepy. Where's Brave Heart?"

I wrapped her baby blanket around the little bear and tucked him under her arm. She went to sleep, smiling and rubbing the trim on her blanket.

---

"Mom, Mom, Zoe has something to show you."

"I paint portraits called EnergyArt." She held up an eight-by-ten picture with red, pink, purple and yellow swirls. Toward the left was an orange abstract figure.

"That's Brave Heart Lion!" I rushed over to get a closer look. "Look how you captured his essence. Did Angie tell you how important he is to her?"

"No, she never said a word. I just saw him lying there while she was sleeping and knew he was very, very important in her life."

"Read what she wrote for Brave Heart, Mom."

I read out loud. "Your guardian angel bear is orange, signifying an important relationship, a watchful eternal one."

"Minky has always been watching over me."

Minky was Will's name for his grandmother, Rob's mother. By the time Will was born, she had retired from teaching and had battled cancer for ten years. Will loved visiting her and always ran to her and gave her a big hug. When his seizures began, she sought out the best neurologists in NYC and in Westchester County, where she lived. She paid the thousands they demanded up front that the insurance wouldn't cover.

She had given Will the little Care Bear when he was a baby and he had never been without it. A few years ago Angie had called from college in a panic: "Did I leave Brave Heart? I can't find him in my suitcase." Sure enough, he had fallen behind the bed and had to be overnighted to her dorm room. She simply could not exist without Brave Heart Lion.

In the final days of Minky's life, Will visited to say goodbye. During the next few days, Brave Heart was never out of arm's reach. Rob, his brother and sisters kept watch by their mother's side, and we were expecting the call at any time. We had a Taekwondo test, so we were leaving our house to drive to the do jang; he tucked Brave Heart in his gym bag.

"Mom, look at that beautiful white bird in the front yard." A dove was alone in the rock garden. He didn't move as we crept up close. "Look at those fancy feathers; I've never seen anything like it."

"It's a type of show bird; it must have escaped from someone's home. It's beautiful."

"Look at its legs, they're all streaked with red, like Minky's legs looked the last time I saw her. Mom, do you think this is Minky coming to say goodbye?"

"I think you're right, Will. Tonight we'll call Dad to see how she's doing."

That night when Rob called, I said, "I know. She died about noon, right?"

"How did you know?"

"A white dove was in the garden. Will said it was Minky coming to say goodbye and to tell him she's at peace and she'll watch over him."

Dr. Bowers had told us that the surgery was more difficult for the younger patients than for the older ones. She explained that the younger ones have blood vessels and nerves that are more sensitive; therefore, they have more pain and have a more difficult recovery overall because the skin is not as elastic.

And it had proven to be true. Angie's roommate was fifty-two, was alert and lively within three hours of the surgery; she was out of bed walking all over the hospital two days later. She said she had very little pain.

Angie was crying and moaning from the pain for several days. She had nausea, dizziness, and minor complications and could barely get out of bed, much less walk around. She was miserable, and didn't want us around.

Robert and I checked on her each morning. One day I was sitting with her while she slept. Rob had left to get coffee. He had been gone close to an hour.

"Psst, Rhonda, come here," he whispered from the door.

"What is it? What's wrong?"

"You won't believe this. Remember when we were in the waiting room at Dr. Bowers' office and we saw that real cute young woman with her parents? Well, I just met her dad. She had the same surgery as Angie! We talked forever. It was so nice to finally meet somebody who has been through all this. He said his wife really wants to meet you. Here they come."

We hugged and cried together, exchanged email addresses and shared horror stories. They had driven eight hours to get there, had their whole family with them and were staying in a hotel. "You got the Robinson Avenue house, you are so lucky. We tried but you already had it. She's really feeling bad. Dr. Bowers told us the younger ones have the most pain. And I can't believe your insurance is paying. Ours already denied it. But we felt that she had to have the surgery."

Since that day we have kept in touch. It's a blessing to know that we are not alone on this journey. Our stories are very similar. They both had experienced the same fears, guilt, confusion and anger that we had felt.

After we left the hospital each day, we spent hours wandering around Trinidad, shopping for the grandchildren, eating at every restaurant in town and doing a little sightseeing. Later we would take Angie anything she needed and watch her sleep. It was a very long hospital stay.

It was difficult seeing her lying there. She hadn't shaved for a few days and her beard was growing in. She had begun electrolysis a year earlier, but with her school schedule and so many other things to do, we hadn't been able to finish the beard. It's a long process; each hair has to be zapped at least three or four times. It can take up to 100 hours to clear a beard. She was scrupulous about always covering it with makeup, so I had no idea how heavy it still was.

"Dad, why is Mom crying?"

I quickly dried my eyes. "You're awake. How you feel?"

"My crotch hurts. Isn't that great! But listen Mom, I'm really pissed about my beard. All the other girls had laser treatments instead of electrolysis and the laser takes the beard away. They don't have hair. It doesn't grow back for a few years, they said. And because it takes a lot less time, it actually cost less."

"But, but," I stammered, "I thought only electrolysis was permanent, not laser." Thinking, "Oh God, I made another big mistake. How many times have I screwed up with this whole ordeal?"

There is so much research required to cross over from male to female. A transsexual has to learn how to dress and to act feminine, how to interact with people, how to change the sound of the voice. It takes years to prepare for and to actually go through this most difficult human journey. Being a transsexual is difficult enough, but for a young person starting in the teens, it's a daunting task. Robert and I had done research for years and had helped as much as possible, but there's a lot to learn. The "name change thingy," as Angie called it, was where I screwed up big time.

I thought that I had read all of the info concerning name change, what New York State requires, what Social Security requires. I thought I understood the processes for all different reasons for name change. I thought I had read somewhere that the Declaration Letter was a legal document that allowed name change for Social Security the same way a marriage license allows for name change, and that it doesn't need to go through the state court system. Well, I was wrong. As we found out two days after Angie got out of the hospital, when we went to the SS office in Trinidad to get her gender and name changed.

"I told you we needed to have my name legally changed by the county court, but you said we would take care of it after the surgery at the Social Security office," she hissed through clenched teeth as she stomped back to the car.

"I thought we could, I don't know how I could have been so wrong. I'm truly sorry. It was a mistake."

"I needed to get the new Social Security card; I have this modeling job lined up under my new name. I need to work. You know that I want to be a model. I need to get a job and earn some money." She collapsed in the back seat sobbing. "I told you! I told you!"

"Angie, stop screaming at your mother right now. You hear me?" Robert yelled. "It was a mistake, but it can be corrected. As soon as we get home, we'll write up the papers, get it to the County Court and it will be done in a couple months. You don't need to be working right now. You need to get well. This will be taken care of. Do you understand?"

She had calmed down somewhat. "I just felt that I needed to get a job as soon as possible."

"No, you don't. Not this summer," Robert continued. "You'll have a new name, new ID card and new Social Security card within a few months. Ok? We'll get it all taken care of."

Robert has always been the DMZ for Angie and me. I always try to do too much for her. And then when it goes wrong, I freak out and we get into a pissin' match. At least now, as Angie says, we have the same pissin' equipment.

After Angie was discharged from the hospital, we stayed in Trinidad for another week, to make sure there were no complications and to give her time to prepare for the trip home. I sent Robert up into the mountains of Colorado for a three-day fishing trip. He came back refreshed and happy, with a balloon that said "It's a Girl."

# Chapter 28
# Laser headache

Within weeks of the surgery, we noticed a transformation in her outward appearance—she stood taller and walked proud. She smiled all the time. She was relaxed and looked comfortable. She let her long dark hair dry naturally into a soft flip. And she mentioned that she wanted me to take her shopping. "I want to change my style, try some other colors. How do you think I'd look in green? It's weird to actually feel happy. And you won't believe this, but I'm not going to wear makeup today. Or dry my hair. I'll just go natural. I'm a girl, I'm happy and I have nothing to prove. And one more thing, I'm glad the name change thingy worked out the way it did, I really need the three months to recover. I don't need to get a job yet. You were right; I need to give myself plenty of time to heal. I have the rest of my life to get a job. You know something else, I'm glad I went through this transition, I'm glad I was born a boy, 'cause now I really appreciate what I have. If I had been born beautiful, I wouldn't appreciate it. I've never had any regrets or second thoughts. And at first, I didn't even know about the Standards of Care or what that whole procedure was, I just did what was natural to me, and it was all the right stuff. And you know what else, I'm proud my last name is going to be Williams, to honor the little boy who kept me safe all those years. So it's good we didn't change the name before."

I was beginning to wonder if she was going to pause long enough to take a breath. I had never heard her talking so much. Usually it was short sentences, or grunts or one-word replies. And by naming herself Angela Williams, she stated that she was honoring the memory of Will. She had reconciled her male and female personas.

She was two weeks post operative; we were home in New York, still reeling from the Colorado experience. I had finally gotten a good night's sleep, my first in at least a month.

In the hospital, I had promised Angie that we would look into laser hair removal as soon as we got home. So we found a center in Poughkeepsie and were scheduled for her consultation. She completed the medical form and we waited patiently.

"So, Angie, I see that you have epilepsy," the technician began.

"Yes," said Angie with a puzzled look. "I have epilepsy, but my seizures have been controlled for many years. I don't have them now."

"Unfortunately, we can't perform laser on anyone who has ever had seizures. With each pulse of the laser there is a bright flash of light which can trigger seizures."

"But I don't react to flashing lights. I was thoroughly tested, I spent two weeks in the hospital, they tested me and I don't react to flashing lights," Angie was pleading, her voice shaking and her lips quivering as she fought back tears.

"What if we get a medical clearance from her neurologist?" I asked.

"No, I'm afraid not; this office is very strict. You may find another office that will do that, but we can't do it here."

⚡

She was banging her hands on the dashboard and screaming. "I should never have told them about the seizures. I thought that was a little strange that the first question on the medical questionnaire was have you ever had a seizure. I know that I don't react to light. Why won't they listen to me? It's my life. Why would they care if I have a seizure?"

On the next consultation, I didn't watch her complete the questionnaire. She had three sessions over the next few months, without seizures, which totally cleared her face, and she was very happy. Of course it began to grow back, which we had known it would, but now she goes to Linda on a regular basis, as it grows back in a little at a time. And now the electrolysis permanently kills the follicles.

What I learned from this beard-clearing episode is that laser and electrolysis are best used in combination to get rid of the beard. And sometimes the patient knows more than the technician about what is best for her body.

# Chapter 29
# Surgical artwork

With any surgery there's always the possibility of complications. When we checked out of the hospital, the discharge instructions warned of possible problems. We had stayed in Trinidad an extra week just to make sure Angie was able to travel and had no problems. Living two thousand miles from the surgeon presented all kinds of potential complications.

"Mom, I don't think I'm healing right. I've started bleeding again near the sutures."

"Alright, get the papers and let's read everything."

We read through all the papers and Angie decided to call Robin, the office manager, who was on call. We got a call back immediately and they talked awhile. I was ready to take her to the emergency room, but after talking with Robin, she felt everything was progressing normally.

Her recovery continued without incident for a few weeks. I thought she was OK and she seemed fine. A few months later, she was distressed. She came to me crying and said she needed to see a gynecologist.

"Do you need to go to the emergency room?"

"No, I don't think so. I just need to see a gynecologist. Something just isn't right."

I found a list of gynecologists and left instructions for her to call them and make an appointment as soon as possible. I arrived back home after work to find her in tears. "They can't see me for another week or two. I really need to go soon."

"OK, listen. You have to make a decision. I can take you to the emergency room, or there's an urgent care center near here. It's your call. Get ready and we'll go now."

"The urgent care center is probably fine. I just need to see someone."

We walked in just a few minutes before closing. She was shaking while she completed the paperwork. I had no idea what was wrong. She wasn't very talkative and I had no idea how to help her.

I had gathered the papers from Dr. Bowers so she could explain her surgery to her new gynecologist, who might need to contact Dr. Bowers with questions.

I waited anxiously. She came out from the appointment all smiles.

"Is everything OK?"

"It was really nothing, I guess I overreacted. But you'll never believe what she said. She said she would never have known it wasn't a real one if I hadn't told her. Can you believe that? She said she had never seen the surgery, I was the first she had ever seen, and that Dr. Bowers must be an artist! An artist! Those were her words. I guess it does look real, huh, Mom?"

Shaking my head and laughing, "Well, that is definitely good news."

# Chapter 30
# Legal beagle

"Where you goin'?" Angie had on her Rollerblades and was heading out the door.

"Into New Paltz to meet some friends for sushi."

"Great, have fun."

When we left our off-the-grid home, Rob wanted to find a place that was private, with acreage. Will requested a long paved driveway for Rollerblades and all I wanted was a house as far away from that barn-conversion project as I could get.

I walked into the living room with the open beam wood ceiling and the stone fireplace. I didn't need to see any more. It was love at first sight. I drifted dreamily through the little house, up the spiral stairs to the master bedroom with huge walk-in closets and bath. Nothing was going to stop me from getting this house.

I patiently waited on the deck off the dining room for Rob to inspect every corner of the house and walk the full length of the five acres along Black Creek. Will had already put on his Rollerblades and was zipping up and down the paved driveway.

We made an offer that night. The realtor told us that the owners were shocked because they thought I didn't like the house. Since I only walked through it once and then stayed outside for the rest of the visit, they assumed that I had no interest.

No, I didn't like the house. I loved it. I felt at home immediately and was ready to move in. It was more than we had hoped for. It not only had the five acres, it was connected to hundreds of acres that could never be developed. It was built up on a top of a rock and could barely be seen from the road, two hundred yards away. It connected to the rail trail where Will would be able to Rollerblade, or ride his bike into Highland or he could also easily go the other way three miles into New Paltz, a cute little college town.

We often wished we could move this house to North Carolina. It was a custom-built home; the foundation was built into the rock. In the woods were miles of stone walls from a hundred years ago, snaking through and down to the waterfalls on the Black Creek.

Angie was recovering from the surgery. She was making new friends at the college and beginning her new life. She told me that it was such a relief not to have to explain that she was a transsexual.

"Now you're a legal beagle," I teased her.

"And I don't have to tell anyone unless I want to. Of course I would never be intimate with anyone unless they knew the whole story. I just want to enjoy my new life without talking about the past. Just talk about normal things that everyone talks about. Oh, yeah, I'm going to meet Alan's parents this weekend."

"That's nice." "Wait a minute," I thought. "What did she say?" "Did you just say you're going to meet his parents?"

"Yeah," she grinned sheepishly. "You know we've been best friends for years, but believe me, we're taking it slow. We don't want to ruin our friendship."

I leaned my head against the kitchen window, watching her roll down the driveway toward the future. Toward the life she had planned for herself.

# Chapter 31
# Allison's lament: I'm your daughter, too

I'm not a people person. I like to be around people, to watch them, read about them, help them, but I'm more engaged with projects, numbers and thoughts than with people. Unfortunately, those are not the qualities of a good mother. And any parent of a special-needs child knows that the other children in the family are shortchanged.

Crystal was twelve and Ally was nine when Will was born. He had surgery at three months and began having seizures soon afterward. My life was pretty much controlled by his many needs from then on.

Crystal and Ally were independent, self-assured young girls, and I always thought they were doing well making their own decisions. They were also doing very well in school. We definitely had our share of teenage problems which I felt we worked through. I watched them graduate high school and college with honors, begin careers, marry and start families.

I wanted to have a close relationship with them; we visited and they visited us as often as possible. Both of them had been like second mothers to Will. Crystal always bought him clothes, gave him advice and had him stay with her in the summer. Ally took him to Disney World and on a Disney cruise. But in the last few years they had drifted apart. Neither of them had spent much time with Angie.

The girls tried to accept their baby brother's transition, but they had a very difficult time understanding. They felt

Angie was manipulating us and that we shouldn't pay for her treatment and surgery.

After the terrible Christmas confrontation with Angie, when I had felt totally blindsided by my ignorance of how she felt about me and how I had treated her, I felt that I needed to connect with Crystal and Ally and see how they felt about having me as a mother.

And they let me know in no uncertain terms my failures as a mother. They said that they had felt unloved, that I was distant and detached, not involved in their lives and activities. And of course, I was too involved with Angie. Nothing they said surprised me. They deserved much more from a mother.

"She's not your only daughter—I'm your daughter, too!" Ally was sobbing and shaking her fists at me. "Did you hear me? I'm your daughter, too! And Crystal is your daughter. And you've never, ever been here for me or Crystal, and to make it worse—you're not here for your grandchildren."

It was bad enough that I was Mommy Dearest, but I was also Grand Mommy Dearest. I felt that everything I had thought about myself was wrong. I didn't know how I could have been such a bad mother, so totally unresponsive to my children's needs. But I vowed I would do whatever I could to try to mend my relationships.

Standing in judgment before one's daughters is a humbling experience. Hearing how I had failed them brought me to my knees. We all know that hell hath no fury like a woman scorned, but, believe me, the fury of daughters scorned is the worst. It must certainly be good preparation for the final judgment day.

I began praying for forgiveness for hurting my children. I asked for wisdom and understanding and to find ways to make the relationships better. "Help me fight my greatest enemy—myself." And I asked them for forgiveness.

Ally had suggested a family reunion. I planned for months and months. I bought backpacks for the three grandchildren and filled them with necessities for the weekend. "Look at all this stuff." I was showing Rob all the gear, spread out on the bed. "Each one has a disposable camera, sunglasses, an insect catching kit, travel toothbrush and toothpaste, tissues, sunscreen, first aid kit, water bottle and games. Did you notice? It's all color-coded. Jim's stuff is blue, Billy's is orange and Maddie's is pink. You think they'll like it?"

"I bet they'll think it's Christmas. What's all this other stuff?"

"Each of the adults has a travel bag with lotions, soaps, coffee, tea, a mug, honey, shampoo, deodorant, hair spray, insect repellent and razors. I just love all those little travel size products. You think it'll be fun?"

"No doubt, we will have a great time."

"So, I figure we'll go to the farm up the road for apple picking, then we'll have a cook out, and we'll drive to Red Hook to visit the farm. It's going to be busy."

<hr />

The second day of their visit was the trip to see the barn where they had grown up. Ally had mentioned that she wanted to show her boys where we had lived. "Look at all the butterflies," said Billy. "Were they here when you lived here?"

"We had birds, butterflies, pheasant and deer—just look at all these flowers and the fields we played in." Ally was showing them all her favorite play areas. "And we had to walk all the way out to the road to go to school. I had to walk a mile through snow! I had to carry in firewood to keep the fire going all the time. We couldn't let it go out. And before we got running water, I had to bring in water from the well. Mom used to tell people, 'Yes, we have running water, the girls run out every day and bring it in.'"

I watched as she proudly showed them where her room had been. "Look! Look! The glow-in-the-dark stars are still on the ceiling. Wow! I can't believe they left my stars on the ceiling."

The reunion was a success. Unfortunately, Crystal and Angie couldn't come, but we kept them on the phone as we had each adventure, so they shared the day with us.

Over the next few years, each time I visited, I set aside time for each one. Crystal and I went to lunch and the spa. Ally and I sat together with tea and talked for hours. I asked questions about their lives and dreams, their fears and failures.

We had camping trips with the grandchildren in "Nana's camper." We played games and talked for hours. They liked going to campgrounds or just parking in the yard. All three grandchildren said the nights in the camper were some of the best ever.

I began a writing campaign to the grandchildren. For the last three years, I have sent them mail at least twice a month. I send stickers, games, cards, homemade cards, baseball cards, and origami papers, anything that will fit in an envelope. The last time I went for a visit, they came running over, hugged me and said, "Nana, we're so glad you're here."

Allison was our golden child. Easygoing, no medical problems, good in school, athletic, she never gave us any problems growing up. She was independent and had lots of common sense, so we allowed her to make her own decisions, and she always knew what she was doing.

She adored Rob, but then again, with his Robin Williams personality, most people love him. She put him totally over the edge when she asked him to adopt her; he threw a party to rival a wedding. She was always his daddy's girl. She attended SUNY Maritime, a military academy on the Throggs Neck peninsula where the East River meets Long Island Sound. She graduated with a mechanical engineering degree and a commission in the Coast Guard. She was also an officer in the Merchant Marines and shipped out on oil tankers for a few years before she married and had children.

While she was in college, we would occasionally meet in NYC. I was waiting for her at our usual meeting spot one day, when she came hurrying in. "I couldn't remember where she was. I must have stopped every security officer and said 'Where's Joan of Arc? Where's Joan of Arc?' They kept telling me different ways to go, but finally I'm here. And she's still wonderful. What is it that you like about this picture, Mom?"

"Everything, really. But I also think she looks like you. She has deep penetrating blue eyes, light brown hair, and that look on her face always reminds me of the way you look when you talk about Will and Crystal. You always seem to be so concerned about them, but just can't quite figure them out."

She and Crystal hated each other until they became adults and then became the best of friends. Now they talk on the phone daily and visit each other for every holiday. She loved her baby brother and had taken him to on a Disney Cruise when he was about thirteen.

"Oh God, Mom," Ally had called from the ship in a panic. "We were sitting at the dinner table and all of a sudden, he just fell over. I didn't know what to do. I got him back to the cabin and he's sleeping. Does he do this a lot?"

"Yes, dear, it's just a manifestation of his seizures. Is he taking his meds? Not that they help much, but make sure he takes every dose."

"We've been really good about that, I remembered everything you told me. But now I see why you were so upset and afraid to let him come with me. I just thought you were being overprotective. How do you deal with this?"

"Not very well, I'm afraid. But listen, I'm sorry you're having a problem; he should be OK when he wakes up. He probably won't remember anything. Just keep an eye on him."

She and Crystal were both very good big sisters. They adored him; he was just so sweet and had so many problems. But they sure didn't know how to deal with Angie.

―⊩―

"So, Mom, how is she doing? Has she recovered from the surgery?"

"She's on the mend physically. Emotionally, not as well; a few weeks after the surgery she was a wreck. She seemed angry at the world. She started a blog and was blasting every friend and family member. Maybe it's the hormones, but she was a real bitch. I couldn't believe some of the things she was saying about her friends. She said they weren't being honest. She went on and on about how she had been betrayed—by everyone she had ever known. It just wasn't logical. Then I realized that she no longer had testosterone, and she may have been flooded with estrogen. And then as quickly as it began, it was over. I guess her hormones became regulated."

"Yeah, when I talked to her while she was in the hospital, she was so arrogant. She seemed to think you paid for the surgery to try to make up for her bad childhood."

"We felt that the surgery was necessary; we couldn't have a daughter living with male genitals."

"I guess you created a monster."

"Seemed that way for awhile, but then she must have gotten it out of her system, or the hormones balanced. She's very calm now. She doesn't argue. She took her blog down. She listens and takes advice. She apologizes and accepts criticism. She does her chores every day. She's looking forward to going back to school. She reminds me of you when you were growing up. And by the way, how are you doing? Do you think I'm doing enough to be a grandmother?"

"Oh, Mom, the boys are all about Nana. 'Look what we got in the mail from Nana. Look what she sent for Easter. Didn't she give us great things for Christmas? When are we going in Nana's camper again?' Yeah, I'm alright. Thanks for all you're doing."

"How did you grow up without a mother?"

"Grandma was always available to talk. My friends' parents helped me. Dad was great. I just went out and found somebody to talk to."

"I'm so sorry I wasn't there for you and Crystal. I really want to make it up to you now."

"And you are, Mom. We love you. Just keep doing what you're doing."

# Chapter 32
# Nana's camper

The first time we took the grandchildren camping was an adventure. I had toys, books, musical instruments, games, and coloring books. Rob drove to Chicopee, Massachusetts on the Mass Pike, about halfway from our house to Ally's home. They met there and he said the boys were ecstatic. "We're going in Nana's camper. We can't wait."

Rob had bought the camper for me when I came back from North Carolina after spending the winter with my parents. I was still so depressed and upset about the fact that not only did we have to deal with Angie and her problems, but we were not going to be able to retire and move to our property in North Carolina.

"It's a Jay Feather; I'll pull it behind the truck. Isn't it the cutest thing in the world? Look, this is a queen-size bed, there are bunk beds for the grandkids, and the table also makes a bed. There's a bath with shower, a gas stove, oven, microwave, a refrigerator, and a flat screen TV. And we can put a gate here for Petey and Laiha. Can you believe this?"

No, I could not believe it. I had wanted an RV for years. I hate camping, but I love the idea of getting away from everything, going places with my own bed and with my pugs. "But Rob, there's one small problem. We don't have a truck."

He shuffled, looking at the ground. He grinned sheepishly and bit his upper lip. "Well, what if we trade in the Nissan for a Silverado?"

"You sneaky little devil. You've been trying to figure out a way to get that truck for years. I will never learn. You get your truck because you knew I wouldn't turn down the camper. Pretty clever trick."

"And even though we can't retire, we can take it to our property in North Carolina, or we can go anywhere you want. And guess what I'm going to name it?"

"You're going to name it?"

"Yep, look up here over the door, I made a sign already."

"Crossing Route 32," I read slowly.

"When we step into this camper, we are crossing Route 32 and we cannot talk about Angie, work, problems, money, nothing. This is our getaway. This is our little corner of the world to get away from everything."

Jim and Billy ran into the camper, squealing in delight. "Awesome, Nana. I love your camper. Are we going today?"

"Yes, today we're going to a very special campground made just for kids."

We were soon loaded and drove the few miles to Jelly Stone Campground in Gardiner, New York. We were in heaven on wheels. They rode their bikes around the circle hundreds and hundreds of times. They made ruts in the hillside that they raced down. They swam in the pool, played on the playground equipment, made crafts that they sent back home to Ally to thank her for letting them go camping. There were campfires at night and fireworks. They watched the skydivers falling out of the sky. They played miniature golf. At night we played games and read books.

"I read this book at school, it's one of my favorites," said Jim.

"That's really neat; the woman who wrote this, Mary Pope Osborne, was a friend of mine in high school."

"You know her, Nana?"

"Well, years and years ago, I knew her, but I haven't talked with her or anybody I went to school with since then. That was a long time ago."

"But Nana, you tell us that friends are important. Why don't you see your friends?"

They were right. I should have friends, but I didn't. And I should have been closer to my sisters and my parents. I'd always let Rob make all the connections, and I'd become friends with the wives of his friends, but I had made no effort to make friends or to see people from my past. It's not that I don't like people; I do like them, but it's something about my personality. I often feel that I only have enough energy to deal with my immediate family, my job and my home.

But after Angie's surgery, I had begun to make major changes in my life. Angie has lots of friends. Crystal and Ally have friends. Rob was the world's best friend-maker. "Let's get with the program here!" So I did what I do best. I made a list of all the people I wanted to get in touch with. And that list has been growing ever since, and I keep checking them off.

# Chapter 33
# Mama said that I could be the swan this year

I was backstage at our local community theater in Fayetteville, North Carolina. I was cinching up my purple and black Scottish National tartan skirt. I stretched the black tights up high and then sat on the floor to tie the ghillies. I was slowly crisscrossing the black satin ties when the music to Tchaikovsky's *Swan Lake* began.

My baby sister Evan rushed onto the stage. I jumped up, hopping on one foot. "No, you can't do that," I yelled. "Mama said I could be the swan this year." I stomped my foot and threw down the other slipper.

DING! rang the chime.

"That's my cue, no, no, I'm not ready. Get off the stage, it's my turn. You get to do this part every year. It's my turn. Mama said I could do anything I want to do."

Evan glared at me, stuck out her tongue as she the swan, slowly died on stage.

"Move out of my way," I shouted to her as I hopped on one foot, trying to jam the other foot into the slipper.

"No! No, you're not!" cried Jamey as she shoved me out of the way. "I'm Mama's favorite and this year I'm the swan. You and Evan get to do everything." She raced onto the stage in her Giselle costume.

DING! rang the chime again.

I blinked several times, trying to adjust to the darkness. "I was dancing," I mumbled. I pulled the covers up close to my chin, took a deep breath, rolled over, hugged Rob and scrunched down farther into the down pillow. I exhaled, smiled and closed my eyes.

DING!

I turned off the Zen alarm clock and reached for my stretch yoga pants. I felt in the darkness for my pink, wrap-around Danskin sweater. Tiptoeing down the spiral stair-case, I heard Petey and Laiha whimpering in anticipation. "OK. OK. Be quiet, don't wake Poppi."

Waiting for the pot of white tea to steep, I forced myself into the yoga stretches that I dreaded. I'm basically lazy and hate to exercise. In protest to the thought of my usual stretches, I bent down slowly into a demi plié, then into a grand plié. "Now that's truly muscle memory, I haven't done a ballet move in thirty-five years." I slowly lifted my leg high in the air and placed my heel on the back of a chair. The rhythmic piano music began to play in my mind, leading me through the barre exercises. My body took over and I fell into the routine easily.

Eyes closed, I let the memories flood back. I was sliding down the rabbit's hole into a strange nether-land of muscle pain, blistered toes, pulled muscles and broken ribs from a clumsy dance partner.

I studied ballet for twelve years. My sisters and I studied with our neighbor, who had been a Rockette before she moved to Fayetteville to open a dance school. Mama had lifted the ban on dancing that Baptists had imposed. So we had been allowed to study with Ann.

Years later my youngest sister, Evan and I opened a ballet school. She was the head teacher; I was the lead dancer for the civic theater and the choreographer for musicals. It was magical. It ended abruptly when Evan was seriously injured in an auto accident. We had many very good students, one of whom went on to dance with the San Francisco Ballet company.

Here I was thirty-five years later, totally exhausted from stretches and movements. My untouched tea was cold.

I began to pull out my photo albums from years earlier. I breathed deeply the musty smell of my scrapbook. I was looking for any remnants of time when body, mind and spirit were blended into a harmonic, meaningful life.

I was staring at the pictures of Evan. I found some of Jamey. She and I are the middle girls. We have never been close; we just kind of existed side by side. And we fought a lot. She's blonde with blue eyes, looks like Daddy. I look like Mama. I was staring at the picture of Jamey in her long flowing ballet skirt. She was tall in her point shoes; her hand was reaching toward a prop on the stage. Her deep blue eyes were in an ethereal gaze, as if she were listening to some mysterious voice.

With a start I dropped the picture and feverishly began to flip through my scrapbook to the pages that held prints of my favorite art work. There she was, gazing from my print of Joan of Arc, with the exact same pose, same stance, same lift of her arm, same gaze—the girl I thought looked so much like Ally—that girl was Jamey!

I knew then that it was time to mend my relationships with my family. I wanted to be a better daughter, a better sister. I wanted to spend time with all of them. I wanted to go home.

I wrote Jamey and told her I was coming home for a visit. She called me and said that she and Evan were spending time together since Evan had moved back home. I knew then that we were all headed in the right direction.

We decided to have a reunion. I traveled to North Carolina to be with them. We laughed and joked and began to make plans for the future. All four of us were together for the first time in many years. We had a portrait made to give to our parents. We went out to eat, watched movies, took Mama shopping—and of course, she shopped till we all dropped. She can still run circles around all of us.

Jamey Lynn showed us a new way to fry okra. Ruby Ann taught us how to make Christmas ornaments out of seashells. Evan took us to the thrift stores she had found at the beach. And I—well, I tried to behave. I didn't bite, scratch, kick or punch, which they said was a relief, since I always did those things when we were growing up.

"I did not!"

"You did so!"

"Did not, either!"

# Chapter 34
# Be my friend

After Angie's surgery, when life seemed to have calmed down, I began to think about friends. I was watching Dr. Oz one afternoon, and he said that to be healthy you must connect with your friends. I decided that maybe he and my grandchildren were right. I got out my list of friends that I had begun compiling a few months earlier and started to seriously plan to become a real friend to each one on my list.

Angie was well on her way to recovery. I had some free time. I was trying to be healthy and had begun an exercise program. I had recently joined the fitness center and started swimming again.

Some of my earliest memories are of swimming. Mama always said that I took naturally to water. We spent lots of time in the summers at a lake near Elizabethtown, North Carolina. The water was crystal-clear; I could see all the way to the white sandy bottom. I spent hours and hours swimming around the piers. Back in those days, getting a tan was a contest to see who could get the darkest. I always won.

"Look at you," Mama always said, "you look just like a Lumbee Indian princess."

Mama was a full-time homemaker in the 1950s, like most mothers were then. But she had a vivid imagination and filled my head with stories of life in North Carolina, where our family had settled hundreds of years before. "We wanted to help the Indians."

Despite the glamorous life my mother depicted of a Lumbee Indian princess, I knew it wasn't true. The Lumbee

Indians of North Carolina, possibly the descendants of the Lost Colony, were much maligned, and have fought for years to be recognized as a tribe. They continue their fight today. Maybe today there are Lumbee Indian princesses. I sure hope so.

It was not until I was much older that I understood her stories of kindness and goodwill toward all, and her genuine Christian desire to help the downtrodden. She is truly a dedicated Christian who spends hours and hours volunteering for the homeless, the veterans who languish in the hospital in Fayetteville, the underprivileged. Mama still gives more time to others than she spends on herself. When she and Daddy went to Ghana as missionaries, I finally understood her need to help. She felt the pain of their suffering. She wanted to do her part to make it right. I admire her and Daddy for their devotion to others.

Daddy was the vice president of a small railroad that served Fort Bragg, a large military reservation near our home. In the 1970s it was bought by a much larger freight carrier. The new owners told him that his job was secure, but they would have to lay off all the laborers. He told them, no: if they let the laborers go, they would have to lay him off, too. So for a year until he turned sixty and could collect his railroad retirement, he and the laborers looked for work and collected unemployment.

I tried to remember when I had done anything to help someone outside of my family. Besides giving money, when did I volunteer to help anyone? I couldn't remember a single time. I felt shame and embarrassment that my parents had set a perfect example and I had done nothing.

I joined the Auxiliary of St. Francis Hospital and volunteered to work in the gift shop, I began to make crafts and donate them for fundraisers. I sold plants and flowers to raise money for the hospital. I became a sponsor for two children through the Christian Children's Fund. I made gift bags with school supplies to send to orphanages in Russia.

I'm in the DAR, so I made lap robes for veterans in the hospitals. I found that the best way to lift one's spirits is to help someone else.

And then I started swimming seriously again. When I was seven years old, I had joined a swim team. At first it was synchronized swimming, but later I started racing. Every year, until I turned sixteen and cheerleading became my new love, I swam competitively. And every year I was on the same swim team with Patsy Bowles.

It was a friendly competition; she was naturally talented and didn't have to work nearly as hard as I did. We weren't the closest of friends but we had quite a history together. I can't even hear the word "swim" or "hundred meters" without thinking of Patsy.

Soon after I returned to swimming, I heard that Patsy had died. Part of my history was dead, part of me had died. There had been other classmates who had died—but Patsy was so directly tied to my life, that she took part of me with her.

I wanted to get it back. As I began the laps at the local fitness center, she filled my thoughts. We always wore matching black tank suits with a diving logo. I researched the Web for the tank suits. I ordered competition one-piece swim suits, goggles, and swim cap. I swam two to three times a week, just back and forth, back and forth.

I was a little sad that diving wasn't allowed at the fitness center. I really wanted to do a racing dive, race down to the other end, just like when Patsy and I were kids. It was good to swim but it just wasn't enough.

One day I overheard someone mention the Senior Empire Games. I hurried home to research the games and discovered the website. I was so excited; I could barely complete the application.

"Rob, Rob, check your calendar. Are you free June 9th to the 12th? We're taking the camper to Cortland."

"We are? What in the world for?"

"I'm swimming in the Senior Empire Games. I'll get reservations at an RV park; we'll take Petey and Laiha. Won't that be fun?"

He gave me a big hug. "It's so good to see you laughing and excited about something. I'm a little confused, though; do you know how to swim? I've never even seen you in a swimsuit. What's this all about?"

"Of course I know how to swim. I was a champion swimmer. Patsy and I swam together for years and years, but now...but now..." I sobbed. "She's gone and I have to swim for her."

"We'll go. Don't worry. We'll have a great time."

I graduated from Fayetteville Senior High School in 1967; it's now called Terry Sanford, named after our classmate Betsy Sanford's father, who was governor while we were in high school. I had never been to a reunion or kept in touch with friends from school, except to see some friends from my church and to attend a reunion of the cheerleaders and other girls. I was planning to move back to North Carolina within a few years; I decided I should make some effort to contact some friends.

Over the last few years, there have been occasional emails sent out to a lot of us: I always read them with interest but never responded. Part of my problem was that I was afraid someone might ask about children, and I wouldn't know how to respond.

The emails began to arrive more frequently, but most of them were to announce the death of another classmate. Within twelve months, there were six deaths. I decided it was time to take action. I sent an email to my classmates announcing that in memory of Patsy, I would be swimming in the New York Senior Empire Games. I challenged them to do some type of activity to honor other classmates.

And they responded. Some planned golf tournaments and other activities to honor our late classmates. We began to email frequently, and I began to feel that I had friends.

I mentioned that I would be in North Carolina for a few weeks, and within a week there was a luncheon scheduled. And then someone started an online prayer group for our classmates who were facing illness. I was becoming part of a group that I had never really been apart from. We were all in our sixties and reaching out to some of the closest friends we had ever known in life.

I was consciously working to become a healthy person. I was developing friendships. Rob and I were enjoying trips in the camper. I was spending time with my grandchildren and my children. And it all came about because of Angie and her sisters. They taught me how to live a true life. Angie, Crystal and Allison tolerated me with all my shortcomings. They had survived living off-the-grid; they had known divorce, poverty and social isolation. They have overcome more adversity than a lot of people see in a lifetime. They are steel Animulas, small young animals facing huge challenges.

Call out your Valkyries, fallen Animula
Backtrack and loop, you, who hoped to play house.
Wait underground, pray, invoke your deep strength
While he rages, Indigo Hank, 'gainst arterial light.
Howl, Animula, at your innocence dark
Ash on the scrolled key hastens the flow
Scowl at the outcast
Sneer at the teller
Resurface from behind, attack with full force
Glare at the bones, the knowledge will come.
Cross the bridge to Valhalla with your crimson soft belly
And armored, Steel Animula, now bask in your light.

# Chapter 35
# Opposites attract

One night during the winter after Angie's surgery, I awoke with a start. I thought I heard the back door slam. "Rob," I whispered. His side of the bed was empty. "He's not on call for emergencies," I thought. "Where is he going?"

I grabbed my jacket and hat and ran to the back door. I shoved the door against the snow. "Oh, my God." The heavy wet snow covered my boots and was up to my knees. I could hear branches in the woods cracking and crashing to the ground. In the moonlight I saw the evergreens tipped over, nearly touching the ground. Just then I heard the chainsaw whining in a high crescendo. "Has he lost his mind? It's the middle of the night."

"Stay back," he shouted. "Get in the house. Fill both tubs with water. Find the candles. It's bad. It's real bad."

Wringing my hands and nodding obediently, I turned back just as the huge maple crashed onto our front porch. "Get in the house, now!" he screamed.

Terrified, I raced back. I threw the wet clothes on the floor and began filling both tubs with water. "What else did he say to do? Oh God, what did he say?" I stood trembling. I was paralyzed. "What do I do? What do I do?"

My heart was racing. I knew he was all right; he had worked his way through college as a logger in Oregon, so I knew he knew what he was doing. I watched him in the headlights of the truck as he deftly removed the largest branches, and then systematically removed the tree which was just inches from our living room and the power line.

Boom! Boom! The transformer up the street sent fireworks high into the air. I watched the street lights as they flickered one by one into darkness. Boom! Boom! Our lights flickered and then the house was dark. The furnace choked and shut down. The water pump sputtered and was quiet. The only sound was the chainsaw and my labored breathing.

"What did he say to do? The candles, oh yeah, the candles." I felt along the antique sideboard for the emergency candles he had stashed. I found the matches, lit each candle and placed them throughout the house. Then I just sat and watched him for hours, trimming limbs, stashing them in the gully.

The morning light crept over the little cedar that had made such a cute trellis; now it lay destroyed, blocking the driveway. The limbs of the evergreens were strewn across the yard—it looked like a battlefield. Tops of trees covered the ground; their fresh wounds ripped open by the weight of nearly two feet of snow.

Rob struggled into the house with the kerosene heater. "Now listen, we can't leave this unattended. You have to stay close by. I've got to get the one set up in the basement. Then I have to load up the truck with cans to get more gasoline and kerosene. We have the generator; we can use it if we need to. For now, this is fine." He barked orders for a few minutes then left again.

When he came back in, he lit the gas stove and made breakfast. "Now just stay here. Don't try to do anything. I'm going to snowshoe out to see if any place is open and I can get some supplies. We don't need much. I can't get the truck out yet, but I'll get it later."

Yawning, Angie emerged. "Power's off, I guess. Is Dad in high gear?"

"Oh yeah, emergency mode. Thank God he's good at it. He snowshoed out to get a few things, we can't get the truck out yet."

"What're we supposed to do?"

"Nothing. You know Dad. Don't do anything until he tells us. You should have been up in the middle of the night. I was terrified."

"It looks pretty awful. I guess I'll just read since I can't do much else."

Hours later, Rob came back huffing and puffing. "I have to check on the camper and the guesthouse. Don't do anything yet. Here, I got a few things."

"Rob, what's the matter with you? We have two feet of snow, no power for God knows how long, and you went out to buy beer and ice cream? You are just too funny."

"When this is over, I'm going to need it."

He raced around nonstop for the six days we had no power. He wouldn't let us do anything. "Too dangerous. I'll do it."

So for six days, Angie and I read and chatted for hours about life on the farm when we had lived without power. "Remember that time we had three feet of snow?" She was animated telling her story. "It was up to my chest. But we were fine 'cause we had the solar electric. That was great; when I build my house, I'm going to have solar electric, but lots more than we had. I'm too attached to my computer to live like we did. But I'm glad we did it. When do you think Dad will slow down?"

"When it's over, not until then."

The first sign of power was the purr of the water pump, and then the lights blinked. We jumped up and down, screaming. I ran out to give Rob the news.

"Get me a beer, I'm sittin' down." He didn't move for hours while I began to make lists of things I needed to do. I sprang into high gear, washing clothes, running the dishwasher, emptying the spoiled food from the refrigerator. I moved all the frozen food from the outdoor freezer back to the house. I raced around vacuuming and cleaning, humming while he sat and did nothing.

It's our differences that helped us to survive the years with Angie. He kept busy handling all the emergencies and I made endless lists and took care of all the routine tasks that had to be done. When I couldn't handle a problem, he stepped up and took care of it. He kept us laughing with his antics. When he totally fell apart in grief, I was strong enough to carry him. Thank God we are total opposites.

# Chapter 36
# Venturing out into the world

I feel blessed that I've been given a second chance to make up for my children's neglect. I don't know if they will ever forgive me or feel that we are close, but at least I know my failings and will work to be a better mother and grandmother.

We finally had Angie's name legally changed through the county court system. She got a new Social Security card and her New York State Expanded ID card that allows her to travel to Canada, where she hopes to settle. She likes Toronto because it's a major center for communications, which is her major. They also have a reliable public transportation system; since she doesn't drive, she has to choose a large city.

I'm currently working to get her amended birth certificate. What a bunch of bureaucratic red tape that is. The New York State Department of Health requires as much paperwork and medical documentation as the surgeon needed. I sent off a twenty-page packet just the other day and then got a call from them asking when she had legally changed her name. Really? Didn't I send a copy of the court order? Well, yes, they had that but needed more documentation. So I had to send more documentation and still it will take three months. But I digress; I'll leave it for another day.

Angie continues to recover emotionally and physically. She took some time off from school, but is now eager to return. She has begun to ask my advice concerning clothes and makeup. One day we went to the Clinique counter at Macy's for a makeup lesson.

"So, what do you need today, dear?"

"I just thought you could maybe help me with my eyes."

"You have the most gorgeous, clear skin. I can tell you take good care of it, and you definitely stay out of the sun. That's a good thing. You don't need much makeup, sweetie. I'll do your eyes and then all you need is a little lip gloss. How tall are you?"

"Five-six," Angie glanced at me, confused.

"With your long dark hair, skinny frame and exotic looks, you could be a model. Did you ever think of that?"

Angie looked at me and winked.

I sat watching her learn to smudge the grey eyeliner. She chose shadow that made her green eyes pop. She was chatting easily with the salesgirl, totally absorbed in the lesson. I'm sure I was "grinnin' like a chessy cat," as Mama always says.

Her green eyes sparkled and her pink lips spread into a wide smile. "Oh, Angie, our exotic butterfly," I thought. I haven't seen any fishnet since her surgery. She came up to me a few days ago, gave me a big hug and told me she loves me.

"Thank you for helping with all this, Mom. I'm glad we're still buddies."

For Christmas I gave her a pink checkered scarf, purple beret, black leather gloves and a black backpack with pink, yellow and teal plaid. I knew it was a big risk; I was waiting for her to just toss them aside. Since Christmas, I'm sure she has told me at least five times how much she likes all of them. She wears the scarf every day; the backpack is her main school bag now, and purple is becoming one of her favorite colors.

While she's been home with us, she has entertained me for hours with comedy routines. She can mimic Lewis Black, Robin Williams and Brian Regan. She calls me to her computer to show me a new routine by one of them on YouTube, and then every time we pass in the hall she will begin a new routine. Everyday she plays with the pugs and spends hours chatting and laughing with her friends on the phone. I can't help but smile when I hear her broadcasting her commentaries of computer games. She gives the blow-by-blow of the fighters and adds her own rowdy, boisterous outbursts, complete with expletives that could make a sailor blush. She has developed a following of online gamers who regularly contact her and ask her to join their games so she can entertain them with her commentaries.

Our Angie
Jumper dog pal
Black belt buddy
Shopping sister
Luminescent black pearl
White jade little Buddha
Mencken's wit, Emily Dickinson's passion
Brave Heart Lion's tiger
Stealth hunter
Blue bird, exotic butterfly
Phoenix rising
Steel Animula gazing at Met's Joan
Still waters' visionary
With Rollerblades under the sushi bar.

# Chapter 37
# Forty five years to reconciliation

"I'd really like to see where the Hudson River begins." Angie was gazing upriver as we stood high above the water on the Walkway Over the Hudson, an abandoned train trestle recently converted into the longest pedestrian bridge in the world.

"Why don't we plan a trip in the RV? We could all go to the Adirondacks, to Lake Tear of the Clouds; that's where it begins, high up on Mount Marcy." I glanced up at her smirk and one raised eyebrow. "I know you don't like the RV, but it would be fun."

"Not my idea of fun. But we'll see. I might be able to tolerate one night. I'm goin' to jog to Poughkeepsie. I'll be back and catch up with you in awhile."

Smiling to myself, I sighed heavily and propped my elbows on the rail. The scent of sunscreen was all I needed to remind me of North Carolina. I had been home with my family just a few weeks earlier. My sisters and I had gotten together for Easter at the beach, our first time together for Easter in forty-five years. "There's hope for Angie and her sisters to reconcile," I thought. Someday, maybe they'll all get together. They'll have a new beginning like my sisters and I have. It may not be in my lifetime, but I have to hope.

"Beautiful up here, isn't it?" a passerby remarked.

Yes, it is. The majestic Hudson River sparkled with sunlight broken up into millions of diamonds. Looking upriver, I saw the Catskill Mountains and the journey of Angie's life. Her young life had begun with so many tears, so many twists and turns. And here we were, a year after her surgery. Her life had been salvaged out of the ruins just as this bridge had been salvaged.

She had chatted easily as we started our walk across the river. "I'm looking forward to being a teacher. I really think that I can relate to middle schoolers. I've had their problems. I understand them. And I'm glad I've started running again. There's a lot of strategy to long-distance running. Maybe I'll be the coach for the track team and the cross country team."

I was amazed at how far we had come in a year. She never talked about her difficulties anymore. She was glad to be back in school. She was happy, at last. I walked to the other side of the bridge to look downriver toward the Hudson Highlands and to imagine the life she had ahead of her.

The winding river flows toward a sea of possibilities.

# EPILOGUE

"Rob!...Robert!...What are you doing?"

He was wielding a sledgehammer, breaking up the slate steps to our home. "Don't tear them down. You know I love those steps. I can use them to put flowerpots on. We can build wooden steps over here. What's wrong with you, Robert? Have you lost your mind? Talk to me! Are you going to be running around like a maniac with a chainsaw next?"

He leaned against the sledgehammer, slowly wiped his brow and grinned at me. "Fixin' 'em. I'm goin' to fix 'em. Over the last three years, you've transformed this into a stone patio with a stone wall. The least I can do is fix the steps. I'm fixin' 'em. Then we can put this house on the market, retire and move to North Carolina. We're goin' baby. You're going home."

He spent the entire summer after Angie's surgery "fixin'" the slate steps.

And now it's time to go home. Back to my parents and sisters, who have settled within a few miles of each other on the Intracoastal Waterway. Back to visit the homeplace, the plantation that I love.

I'm in touch with my high school friends in Fayetteville. Two of them have summer homes just a few miles from our property at the beach. We're planning reunions and luncheons.

Carol Beth, still practices oral surgery in Cambridge, but we're planning to spend every birthday together. She likes to travel and wants to see North Carolina.

I'm looking forward to spending more time with Crystal and Maddie, who live in North Carolina. Allison and her family promise they will visit.

Angie is in school full-time in New York. She shares a house with four other college friends. We keep in regular contact.

I retired in March 2010 from UnitedHealthcare. Robert retired in September 2010 from New York State, and he's itchin' to buy that fishing boat. He has already joined the Brunswick County Fishing Club where my granddaddy was a charter member.

My sadness has lifted. My life is renewed. I'm my true self at last.

And I'm going home.

⁂

"Please pass the fried okra 'fore I have to fight you and steal it."

"Mama! Evan's hoggin' the okra!"

"If I have to git my switches, your bee-hinds are goin' to burn."

"Run! Evan! Run!"

## THE END